Believe in Tomorrow

Believe in Tomorrow
A Biblical Perspective of
The New Earth

Dr John Dyer

Kingdom Publishers

Copyright© Dr John Dyer 2024

All rights reserved. No part of this book may be reproduced in any form by photocopying or any electronic or mechanical means, including information storage or retrieval systems, without permission in writing from both the copyright owner and the publisher of the book. The right of Dr John Dyer to be identified as the author of this work has been asserted by him in accordance with the Copyright, Designs and Patents Act 1988 and any subsequent amendments thereto.

A catalogue record for this book is available from the British Library.

All Scripture quotations have been taken from the New Kings James version of the Bible

ISBN: 978-1-916801-19-6

1st Edition 2024 by Kingdom Publishers, London, UK.

You can purchase copies of this book from any leading bookstore or at:
www.kingdompublishers.co.uk

For my grandchildren

Aurora and Luís

Books by the same author:

Encounters with God in Brazil: Personal Stories to Amaze and Inspire

Jesus: Dead or Alive? The Evidence

Theology for the People: Empowerment and Liberation

Contents

FOREWORD	1
PROLOGUE	5
CHAPTER ONE A Perfect World	7
How did it all begin?	7
Where is God now?	9
The Watchmaker	11
Is history moving forward?	12
CHAPTER TWO Solitary Earth, but not Alone	13
Here for a reason	13
Nature's ways	20
Celestial visitors	22
The beginning of everything	22
Seen from Outer Space	24
Striking similarities	26
The jewel of creation	28
Why do things exist?	32
CHAPTER THREE A new Earth and a new Heaven	40
How new is new?	41
Where is heaven?	42
Cosmic happenings	45
Return to Eden	50
Here already, but not yet	53
When the lights go out	57

CHAPTER FOUR Beyond Paradise	62
Touching heaven	63
Time and eternity	67
A different kind of kingdom	70
Heaven touches earth	73
CHAPTER FIVE Not so other worldly	85
Doubts and questions	86
How to cross over	93
Where to from here?	98
CHAPTER SIX Are we Alone in the Universe?	102
Is there anyone there?	103
The real Wow factor	105
Good bedfellows	110
What can we do?	112
CHAPTER SEVEN Can I believe?	117
Jesus of history	119
What we know now	123
The planet today and tomorrow	126
Postscript	134
Bibliography	135
Articles consulted:	138

FOREWORD

I met John Dyer, his wife Maria, and their son João Marcos in Antonina, on the east coast of the State of Paraná, Brazil in 1989. John was the coordinator of an association of 17 churches and six congregations, engaging and equipping these churches in the mission of Christ. He has continued this ministry of equipping and training church leaders in Brazil and further afield beyond retirement as a missionary in 2012.

In this latest book, Dyer continues to provide material to support Christians in their discipleship; here exploring a biblical perspective of 'The New Earth' from both a biblical and scientific perspective.

Dyer is following in the footsteps of the first BMS missionary, William Carey. Carey is regarded as the founder of the modern missionary movement. He went to India in 1793 and in addition to his missionary work made contributions to the science, natural history and botany of India. This was in addition to his extensive work as a translator of the Bible into various Indian dialects.

At Serampore College, Carey believed that students should be instructed in India's philosophy, literature, religion, and science together with the Christian Scriptures and Western science. When facing criticism from some of his supporters in North America, he commented: 'Can young men be prepared for the American Christian ministry without science?' (Pearce Carey, *William Carey DD Fellow of the Linnaean Society*, Hodder & Stoughton, 1926, 332). Carey was a pioneer in Christian education recognising the need for pastors to understand their culture and the scientific world.

Since the early nineteenth century Baptist theologians and church leaders have had an uneasy relationship with science, especially in the United States of America. There have been strongly held views, based on an understanding of the scriptures, which are often in conflict with the discoveries of science.

Albert Einstein was right to state that religion without science is blind, and that science without religion is lame (Albert Einstein, *Science, Philosophy and Religion: A Symposium*, 1941), but the deciding factor will be the way in which these two areas are brought together. Dyer recognises that science is presenting an ever-clearer picture of the universe of which we are a part. We are understanding more and more of the complex patterns and structures of the galaxies, of human life, and of the sub-atomic particles that compose all things. Cosmologists speak of the discovery of design and pose questions about purpose. There is a growing weight of evidence to suggest that human life could only have developed on this planet through a unique set of parameters, which were established at the birth of the universe itself, which again suggests purpose, but with the additional possibility of humankind being at the centre of that purpose.

Scientific studies take place for a number of reasons: basic human curiosity; the benefits that come from the use of the Earth's resources and from technological advances; and the search for meaning and truth about the world in which we live. Science is only effective because it describes things the way they are.

The people of the Old Covenant worshipped God as the God of their history, who was also the unique creator of the universe, and Lord of the nations. They presented God as a transcendent creator, yet immanent in the history of the people; God shares a covenant relationship, characterized by grace, with the people. All of creation is the place of God's activity and presence. The story of God's people is one of self-centred rebellion, yet God's promise is the hope of redemption for the whole of creation.

In the New Testament Jesus is the Word, through whom God had created the universe and all of life (John 1.1-5). In the letter to the church at Colossae, the apostle Paul recalls a hymn of the church that expresses the place of Christ in creation, and in the redemption of the church and the world (Col. 1.15-20). Here we find that God is deeply and passionately involved in his world; he is no absentee landlord but is indwelling and incarnate (Col. 1.17). In Christ, God will bring the whole of the universe back to himself, making peace (shalom - wholeness) through the Cross, both on earth and in heaven (Col. 1.20). This radical transformation has already begun through the presence of the Holy Spirit (Rom. 8.19-23). We have a picture of a sacramental universe: all creation is in God; God is in all creation; celebrated in bread and wine.

In *Believe in Tomorrow*, Dyer helpfully places Christian belief and mission in the context of the discoveries of modern science. He critically explores both the discoveries of science and the biblical text and brings them together as complementary rather than conflicting accounts of the world as we know it.

We can express his objective in the words of the apostle John: 'These are written that you may believe that Jesus is the Messiah, the Son of God and that by believing you may have life in his name' (John 20:31).

John Weaver

PROLOGUE

The Preacher said three millennia ago:

> That which has been, is what will be. That which is done is what will be done. And there is nothing new under the sun. Is there anything of which it may be said, "See, this is new"? It has already been in ancient times before us (Ecclesiastes 1:9-10).

So, also, with writing a book. Someone will have said it before; someone will have been there before. But this should not in the least deter us from the task of contributing to the discussion in our own day and for our own generation. Knowledge and understanding are increasing and evolving all the time and we are duty bound to help push the boundaries of knowledge a little further out, however small that difference may be.

Everyone's personal experience is unique to them, but each of these experiences is valid and something from which we can all learn. But we also have shared experiences, although the way we interpret those experiences and respond to them will, doubtless, be as individual as we ourselves are.

It is likely that there are people who will be unfamiliar with what I am about to say and the context in which it is written. And for those who are familiar with the territory and have travelled this way before, there will be different ways of arguing the subject and different responses to the arguments presented. Our individual insights come from different perspectives as we see and appreciate things in different ways. It is not surprising to discover that that theory, with which we have been toiling over time, is not so strange or unusual and that others share our opinion. It can also come as an encouragement and comfort to know that one belongs to a particular school of thought, as this adds to our sense of identity. Where others, to my knowledge, have engaged in the conversation, these will be identified and acknowledged as we proceed.

The Preacher was not one of the world's greatest optimists. But he made a valid contribution from his own standpoint based on a particular *cosmovision* of how the world is. It is in this spirit that this short book is written. It comes in the hope that it will challenge the readers to begin their own journey of exploration into the *new* things that God is doing and, also, sharing with us.

The thinking in this book has developed over time and has led to conclusions, some admittedly provisional, that will trigger no small degree of wonder and amazement.

CHAPTER ONE
A PERFECT WORLD

How did it all begin?

The title of this book indicates that we are dealing with the future of our planet. But this cannot be done outside of the context of the universe of which it is a part. In this book, we will reflect on the vastness of the universe and the comparative minuteness of the planet we call home. I am reminded in the Bible of how it all began. Through the optics and beliefs of the priestly writer, man and woman were created by God, given a garden in which to live, raise a family and prosper. They had everything they needed. They had jobs to do in the garden by way of caring for it so that it could provide for their needs. They had food and employment. Everything that nature could offer was provided for them. Rain and sunshine assisted the earth in the growth of crops. Their lives were stress free; they weren't even aware they were naked. It was the age of innocence.

Everything was blissful. Even work was a pleasure and delight. The days were determined by the rising and setting of the sun, as part of a rhythm of work, rest, and play. But then, one day, they decided to take things into their own hands, to take from God control of their own destiny. From then on, everything changed. They became aware of their nakedness and hid from God, prompting the first ever question that God directed to a human being: Where are you, Adam? This led to a long line of excuses for their behaviour, and a sense of guilt, which they had not known before. And things went from bad to worse. Finally, they were expelled from the garden, never to return.

This, in turn, led to negative consequences for the whole of creation, both spiritual and physical, as decay and disorder set in. The realities we describe are clear to see around us, though their explanation may differ according to whether we choose to adopt a scientific or theological stance when considering these issues. In this book, we shall take advantage of both perspectives, which I believe will provide us with a firmer foundation for the findings we shall later present.

In my own garden in North Wales, there is a wooden plaque which reads as follows: To plant a garden is to believe in tomorrow. Not everyone likes gardening, and to be honest, though this form of exercise is good and healthy and can give much pleasure, gardening can sometimes be a chore, as the grass keeps growing and the weeds return despite all our efforts to suppress them. But the writing on the plaque still rings true.

We plant bulbs in the autumn believing, that once winter has passed, they will bring beautiful colour to our gardens in the spring. Then we sow and plant again in the spring, in the firm hope that our gardens will be full of scented flowers throughout the summer months. That is the sentiment behind the words on the plaque in my garden and, also, the inspiration for the title of this book, Believe in Tomorrow.

There are many reasons why we should and can believe in tomorrow and in this book, we shall be exploring the trajectory of humanity, and also that of our planet. This is not another treatise on global warming, as important as that issue is for us today, and rightly occupying our thinking as never before. Here we shall be contemplating how the word of God and scientific knowledge can be reconciled, leading to many surprises along the way.

Where is God now?

I believe that God is always challenging us to think outside the box. It was Israel's inability to do this that brought about their rejection of the Messiah when he came. Even when we think outside the box, we are still guided by what God has already revealed of himself to us. Throughout history, God has revealed himself to his people. Not all at once, but progressively, bit by bit, as and when God chose, and as they were able to take it in (understand and accept). That is, until *the fullness of the time had come*, when God revealed himself to the whole world in and through his only Son (Galatians 4:4).

This is further developed by the writer of the Letter to the Hebrews who declares as follows:

> God, who at various times and in different ways, spoke in time past to the fathers by the prophets, has in these last days spoken to us by his Son, whom he has appointed heir of all things, through whom also he made the worlds: who being the brightness of his glory and the express image of his person, and upholding all things by the word of his power (Hebrews 1:1-3a).

The revelation of God's glory, though complete, is still to some extent veiled and partial. As the Apostle Paul explained:

> For now, we see in a mirror, dimly, but then face to face. Now I know in part, but then I shall know just as I also am known (1 Corinthians 13:12).

I do think this declaration of Paul is apposite for the present generation. Our knowledge of the universe, though increasing day by day is still limited. There's so much of it that we cannot even observe let alone understand. There are also many situations that we witness and experience in our daily lives that are hard to come to terms with. Death, violence, famine, war and, generally, man's inhumanity to man. Because of these hard facts of life, many have written off God. Others argue that even if there is a God who created the world, he has long since abandoned it and left it to its own devices.

Others still, explain everything from the origin of the universe to natural processes on Earth, without recourse to God. In other words, God is being squeezed out of the conversation, and sometimes for reasons one can understand. But it is also true that some arguments against the existence of God are based on a supposition or theory, which one then sets out to establish as fact.

Francis Schaeffer reminds us, that scientists once believed (though there are many who still do) "that there is a reasonable God, who had created a reasonable universe, and thus man, by use of his reason, could find out the universe's form" (Escape from Reason, p.31).

It is true that modern humans are using their God-given powers of reason to discern the mysteries and origin of the universe, but also to eliminate God from the universe and to place their selves above God. Biblical history has a way of exposing the fallacy of these behavioural attitudes. We end up deceiving only ourselves in thinking we are no longer answerable to God, simply by excluding him from our thinking or denying his existence. This is entirely a matter of choice, of course, for God himself has given us the ability and freedom to choose.

This is at the very heart of what it is to be human, after all. But though we may be able to banish God from our thoughts this can make no difference whatsoever to the ultimate question of whether he is there or not. If we think about it, there are clear parallels here with the first humans who did the very same thing! It would seem we haven't come very far at all or that nothing very much has changed. The picture painted of Eden describes very well the situation in which the world finds itself today. The more we try to achieve autonomy over our own lives, the more we isolate ourselves from the source of our being, the greater the human existential crisis becomes.

The Watchmaker

Returning to the thought that God created the world then stepped back from it. This belongs to a particular philosophical argument for the existence of God and is related to the Argument from Design, that originated with Thomas Aquinas and later followed up by William Paley in 1802. Paley was an English clergyman whose teaching was influential at the time of Charles Darwin.

Paley uses the analogy of the watchmaker, to prove the need for a designer and assembler of such an intricate piece of machinery. He then projects this idea on to the world, particularly in the way that nature adapts to different environments and settings. This idea was used by some to suggest that the watchmaker, who having put all the many intricate parts together, winds it up and then leaves it to run on its own. William Paley, however, did not write to this effect. His analogy of the watchmaker had in mind that the natural processes by which all living things live, adapt, and survive are more complex even than the functioning of a watch. Therefore, these also require a designer or person, or God to assemble their respective working parts, so that they function as intended.

The philosophical arguments that build on Paley's analogy advocate that God, though responsible for the world in the role of creator, is no longer active in the world. But this deals with only half the story because, according to the analogy, for the watch to keep the time correctly it would need to be wound periodically, or if run by battery power it would require the battery to be recharged or replaced from time to time. The watch would, in any conceivable circumstance, still require the occasional intervention of the watchmaker.

No analogy is perfect, and this one is no exception. Nonetheless, the workings of the earth's mechanisms (its seasons and predictable lengths of night and day) and the perfect timing of its celestial journey (the duration of its orbit around the sun and its rotation on its axis) together would strongly suggest and indicate that its maker is actively involved in its day-to-day maintenance.

Is history moving forward?

Our interest in this book is also the *new earth* and its relationship to the present one. As the hour of Christ's return, the *Parousia*, approaches, it is imperative that we are prepared, and that we prepare others for this coming cosmic event.

A friend and colleague of mine once asked me what the principal focus of my ministry was. I replied that it was to prepare the people of God for the return of Jesus. He seemed to like that answer! At the same time, that seemed to me to be a confirmation of what I had thought about ministry all along.

It's approaching Christmas as I write this, and there is a devotional on the YouTube channel of the church where I am a member. The young lady giving the message this morning is talking about God's promise to Zechariah concerning the birth of a son to him and his wife Elizabeth. As the devotional unfolds, it is explained that the promised son would prepare the people of God for the coming of the

Messiah. This son was called John, known throughout the world as the Baptist, who would *turn many of the children of Israel to the Lord their God* (Luke 1:16).

This is for me another confirmation of God's purpose for those of us called to lead God's people in today's world, which is to prepare them for the second coming of Jesus. This is promised by God in a way not dissimilar to the promise made to Zechariah. It is especially noteworthy that both promises were made through the instrumentality of angelic messengers, speaking directly to those for whom the message was intended:

> And while they looked steadfastly towards heaven, behold, two men stood by them in white apparel, who also said, "Men of Galilee, why do you stand gazing up into heaven? This same Jesus, who was taken up from you into heaven, will so come in like manner as you saw him go into heaven"
> (Acts 1:10-11).

This will give some idea of our direction of travel through this book. To put things in context, we will be looking at God's creative and redemptive purposes for the entire planet on which we live, suspended in space as it is, and maintained in its constant celestial orbit by the gravitational pull of our local star, the sun. We will contemplate the earth, as it can be seen from space, thousands of miles away, and why this evoked such a personal response on my part. We will then look at what the Bible has to say about heaven and earth, as we seek to discern its message for us today.

We will do this in a dispassionate way, so as to allow the Bible to speak to us and not the other way round. After all, the Bible is best understood when we allow it to explain or interpret itself; that is in the context of other similar or related passages and texts. The best outcome is when one can balance and reconcile the different passages in the pursuit of a coherent whole. Do not be afraid to let the Bible speak to you; and be brave to take on board what it says.

For many, the Bible is just a history book. That is true in part. There is much history within the Bible and particularly some of its books are clearly historical. However, others are not, because the Bible is a library of different kinds of books, and other literary forms abound, including poetry and prophecy. In fact, the people of Israel saw in the Old Testament three main divisions: the Law, the Prophets, and the Writings.

Interspersed among these was also Wisdom Literature, such as the Books of Job and Proverbs and, also, sagas, including the so-called Joseph saga, which tells of his being sold by his brothers and taken to Egypt; something which later proved to be providential for his family in the outworking of God's purposes for his people.

To those who say the Bible is history, I say a resounding, "Yes". By way of history, the Bible tells us of the times when God appeared to key leaders among his people, in key moments of their journey. Jacob, Moses and Joshua in Old Testament times come quickly to mind. But there was another moment when God revealed himself to all of humanity in the person of Jesus Christ. And he not only revealed himself to us as a momentary experience of his presence; he came to live among us; he drew near to us and moved about among us; he clothed himself in our humanity and returned to heaven taking with him our human form.

God is not remote and absent from human affairs, as hard as that might seem at times. He is still involved in human history in ways spoken of in the Bible, but not always perceived by the world at large. Christmas is a shining example of this, when he came into the world, but the world largely went about its normal business, quite unaware of this fact; the cross is another, when the world turned its back on Jesus and ignored his message.

There is one final moment, yet to come, when God will reveal himself to the world, but not as before, as this book will explain. So make yourself comfortable or tighten your seatbelt, as we journey together into the future to discover what lies ahead and what we ourselves can expect to happen.

For further personal reflection or group discussion:

Why do you think the first humans decided to reject God and go their own way?

Do you agree with the saying: We are nearer to God in a garden than anywhere else on Earth?

Are there similarities between the first humans' desire for autonomy over their lives in relation to God and people today?

What do you think of the analogy of the watchmaker as a proof for the existence of God?

How might we read the Bible to understand its meaning better today?

CHAPTER TWO
SOLITARY EARTH, BUT NOT ALONE

O Lord, our God, how excellent is your name in all the earth. You who set your glory above the heavens! When I consider your heavens, the work of your fingers. The moon and the stars, which you have ordained. What is man that you are mindful of him, and the son of man that you visit him? For you have made him a little lower than the angels. And you have crowned him with glory and honour. You have made him to have dominion over the works of your hands; you have put all things under his feet (Psalm 8:1; 3-6).

Here for a reason

I think we too often take for granted our terrestrial home. We use it and abuse it to extremes. Political decisions are taken at much heralded global forums to curb carbon emissions, but economic pressures continue to stall these. Quite honestly, we have not been the best stewards of God's earth. When God created mankind in his own image he said, "let them have dominion over all the earth" (Genesis 1:26). The rest of creation, the birds of the air, the fish that abound in the sea, the trees and the fields, the cattle and every creeping thing, in fact, the whole earth were put under our control (Genesis 1:26-30). But that control was given intuitively to care for and cultivate, not to damage and destroy.

We should remember that our planet hasn't always been a place fit for human habitation. It is only in relatively recent times that it has become so. In the earliest period of its existence the surface temperature was too hot and the atmosphere unbreathable. Humans have inhabited the earth only in recent geological times. In fact, if we think of the earth as being formed 24 hours ago, human existence would have begun later than 23:59. So, to put things into their true perspective, we have been here for only a tiny fraction of the time since the world began – under a second, in fact (Carnegie Museum of Natural History).

So, if we reduce Earth's age from 4.5 billion years to a single day, we can see that we arrived very late in the day. This does not essentially affect the creation story. In the biblical version, the creation of the world and its inhabitants is divided into 24-hour periods over six days, which is remarkably close in concept to the comparative 24-hour timescale used by the natural history fraternity in the present day!

Moving on, our planet is governed, theologically and scientifically speaking, by the equilibrium and constancy of the universe and the limitations of its own sustainability. The scientific explanation for the former is the gravitational forces of the sun, the galaxies, and the universe at large. Theologically, this is explained by appealing to the power and authority of God at work in the universe.

For our purpose here, the writer to the Hebrews has a way of expressing the relationship of the Old and New Testaments as one of promise and fulfilment respectively, and especially in his understanding of the person of Jesus, his role in the creation of the universe and his unique relationship to the creator God. We pick up the thread of his thinking in mid-sentence, so to speak: "... who being the brightness of his glory and the express image of his person and upholding all things by the word of his power..." (Hebrews 1:3).

This is a reference to the Son of God, through whom the eternal God has revealed himself to the world and through whom also he made the worlds (Hebrews 1:2). The writer's words touch on both who Jesus is and what he does. These two, being and doing, belong together; they cannot be separated. To grasp fully or even in part the story of creation, one needs to understand the relationship between the Father and the Son, as follows: the God who revealed himself through the Son also created the universe with the Son. How else could Jesus have calmed the raging storm and stilled the violent waves of Galilee's unpredictable sea? (Matthew 8:27).

And the writer to the Hebrews is not alone in making such a bold declaration. The Apostle John begins his record of the life and ministry of Jesus with the blast of a trumpet which does two things. It declares who Jesus really was and it states clearly that the worlds came into being through his instrumentality:

> In the beginning was the Word, and the Word was with God, and the Word was God. He was in the beginning with God. All things were made through him, and without him nothing was made that was made (John 1:1-3).

All this was also anticipated by the psalmist long before. The songwriter declares that God's word is to be relied upon, a truth which is reflected in the constancy of the universe, the permanence of Earth, and the continuing existence of humankind. All these exist by him and for him:

> Forever, O Lord, your word is settled in heaven. Your faithfulness endures to all generations; you established the earth, and it abides. They continue this day according to your ordinances, for all are your servants (Psalm 119:89-91).

Unlike the medieval church which understood these words to refer to the fixed position of the planet at the centre of the universe, a view challenged by scientists such as Copernicus and Galileo, our understanding is that they refer to the unchanging nature of God's word by which the celestial bodies are sustained. Theologically, the earth owes its permanence to the will of God made known through his word, of which the whole creation are servants, though, it must be said, human action has served to bring the long-term survival of planet Earth into question in recent years.

On a more encouraging note, the Apostle Paul expresses the point most succinctly in these words: "All things were created through him and for him. And he is before all things and in him all things consist" (Colossians 1:16b-17).

Hopefully, our God-given human intelligence will lead us all to see the damage that has been caused to the planet since the beginning of the Industrial Revolution, and that we will succeed in putting in place measures appropriate to the challenge of climate change in the present day.

Nature's ways

There are scientific and theological explanations for the existence and coexistence of the stars, planets and all the other heavenly bodies, planet Earth and its inhabitants among them. We shall continue to make use of these two different but complimentary approaches to a fuller understanding of our own existence and role in God's creation.

Earth, though predictable in its celestial journey, is subject to internal change, seasonal in the short-term, but also epochal, through successive geological *ages*. Cause and effect are always in play. Nature can usually take care of these variations if we manage to avoid getting in the way of its natural processes. As an incentive to avoid getting in the way, it might help to have a proper and realistic perspective of these things.

Earth is the size of a pinpoint by comparison with the unimaginable enormity of space; in fact, it is beyond comprehension how vast the universe really is. And it is a sobering thought that despite the vastness of the universe, realistically there would be nowhere else for us to go if the earth became uninhabitable. It is estimated from what we know that there are at least two trillion galaxies out there, mostly far beyond our reach and capacity to observe (BBC Science Focus).

Like the universe, which began, according to the Big Bang Theory, at a singularity (an infinitely small point of infinite density), this book project has grown from a single emotional response to an extraordinary image of planet Earth, majestic yet vulnerable, unique yet seemingly insignificant against the backcloth of the cosmos. At the same time, our planet is strikingly beautiful with its tides and seasons, mountains and valleys, even by comparison with Jupiter and its tempestuous storms or Saturn's mysterious rings.

Here on Earth, we live in times of unprecedented climatic turmoil with the increasing volatility of our weather patterns. Across the world, extremes of temperature and rainfall, or lack of it, are making the headlines. These changes in the world's climate are affecting our ability to produce enough food to meet demand, and the world's poorest countries find it hardest to adapt to what is happening around them.

Floods and drought bring destruction and starvation in their wake with increasing regularity. Meteorologists inform us that each successive year is hotter than the year before. The air we breathe is compromised by carbon dioxide emissions as never before, the result of human action significantly altering the atmosphere upon which life on Earth depends. The resultant global warming has progressively increased sea levels, causing the polar ice caps to melt away into the planet's oceans.

Celestial visitors

Changing tack, because of the remote possibility of another catastrophic asteroid impact of the kind that brought about the extinction of the dinosaurs, 65 million years ago, scientists are anxious to study the movement and structure of these celestial bodies. Recently, a NASA probe landed on one such distant remnant from the creation of the solar system and has brought back to Earth small quantities of dust and rock from Bennu, the largest and most significant known asteroid roaming the solar system. Asteroids are thought to contain material from the formation of the planets and their moons. They are also important for our understanding of how the solar system came into being and for the origin of life itself.

There is also a longstanding interest in knowing whether we are alone in the universe. The answers are as elusive as ever, though, apparently, it has now become a case of not if but when other forms of intelligent life will be found; that is, if we are not found by them, first. Whether these alien forms will prove to be friendly or hostile towards us humans, or whether they have achieved a greater or lesser degree of advancement than ourselves, we do not yet know.

The beginning of everything

It has been widely accepted that the universe began with the *Big Bang* when stars were created and flung into space. However, scientific theories have a way of being revised and updated to the extent that as soon as one is established, another pops up and takes its place. Even the Big Bang theory has been questioned in some quarters and replaced with the idea of an infinite universe that had no beginning but continually expands and contracts.

But the Bible is on track when it declares:

> And God said, "Let there be light" (Genesis 1:3).

This view has seemingly stood the test of time. We now know that light came to exist at a point early in time after the universe was created. Scientific talk about the universe is the specific province of theoretical physics and is determined by the laws of physics; that is until one reaches the point at which time began.

Here the laws of physics no longer apply and break down, because at that point we find ourselves outside the laws of physics and, by extension, human knowledge. As a result, the search begins for a new scientific understanding of the origin of the universe, and this remains the continuing quest of cosmologists, many of whom have outstanding reputations. While human knowledge is forever being challenged, its boundaries are continually being pushed back.

The language of Scripture and science, though different, are not necessarily incompatible. It is the opinion of this writer that there is no inherent conflict between creation and evolution, science and theology. As we proceed, we shall be looking at scientific theories based on observation and biblical revelation based on experience. Both require a step of faith, before advancing towards new platforms of certainty.

Starting with the creation stories in the Book of Genesis, these may not have been written by Moses, or if they were, he would not have been there at the time to witness the events described. Modern biblical scholarship is largely of the opinion that they were written during the period of Jewish exile in Babylon in the 6th century BC. The writer or writers (because there are two different versions written in different styles and with different presentations) would have likely put pen to paper to present a Jewish monotheistic view of creation with the purpose of countering the prevailing thought among other Ancient Near Eastern religious belief systems, especially the Babylonian creation stories.

The Jewish account, as presented in the Book of Genesis, would be based on core beliefs passed down from previous generations. Before the Book of Genesis saw the light of day, belief in a creator God was evident from the Psalms and the Prophets:

> Ah, Lord God! Behold you have made the heavens and the earth by your great power and outstretched arm. There is nothing too hard for you (Jeremiah 32:17).

And, of course, Psalm 19:1 to which reference is made elsewhere in this book.

Ruth Valerio explains that the message of the Genesis creation story "is one of hope, peace and confidence in a good God who reigns supreme has created a very good world, with people created to work with him in taking care of it and one another" (Saying Yes to Life, p.xvii).

Seen from Outer Space

On 14 February 1990, from the outer limits of the solar system, the spacecraft Voyager 1 took a snapshot of planet Earth. This photo is famously known as the Pale Blue Dot. According to NASA, Voyager 1 took sixty pictures of the solar system before turning away to embark on its even longer journey into interstellar space. The image of Earth was taken at a mind-boggling distance of 3.7 billion miles (www.sciencenasa.gov).

Another photo of Earth was taken by a crewmember of Apollo 17 on 7 December 1972. This photo goes by the name of *Blue Marble* and is the first photograph showing the entire globe of the earth (taken from an article by Jamie Carter and published on 22 August 2019 for travelandleisure.com.

Both photos inspired wonder and fascination and, for the first time, we could look back at our home and ourselves in the vastness of outer space. For me, one word came to mind, as I gazed upon the second of these two images at a Christmas Eve service: *Heaven*.

The solar system is truly amazing and spectacular, but the ability to view planet Earth in this way evoked another adjective, raised to its highest degree: *Awesome*. Yet not just any awesome (a word used somewhat liberally in contemporary English), but the most awesome imaginable - the most awesome thing ever seen.

It was certainly the most awesome image I had ever seen, and which very few people will ever have the chance to capture on camera. Set in the solid blackness of space, its atmosphere shining blue, its white clouds, and the darker tinge of its continents combining to take one's breath away. So, after that, whenever I thought of heaven, I was immediately drawn to this incredible image, which has forever imprinted itself on the retina of my eye.

As I have said, this image so impacted me that I immediately exclaimed, "Surely, this must be heaven!" We hear something similar said in moments of great joy and blissfulness; *this is heaven on Earth.* But this evocative verbal expression may not be simply a metaphor. From the moment of this stark realisation, I had begun a journey of discovery to find out how true and how literal that might be.

From primordial times, humans have looked heavenward and wondered if they were alone in the vastness of space. Or as we have come to understand it, this ever-expanding universe, like a balloon of infinite elasticity. By modern scientific measurements, the cosmos is currently expanding at a rate faster than the speed of light, although this is relative to the distances involved. The greater the current distance between celestial objects the faster the distance between them increases.

Therefore, we will never be able to see objects that are already beyond what is called the light horizon, because the light from those objects will never be able to reach us. I find that an awe-inspiring reality of the universe, of which we are all part. What was set in motion 14.5 billion years ago is alive and well, so it would seem.

How was it set in motion, who or what set it in motion are the questions which science and theology together can answer. And working together, they can provide a coherent answer in response to the searching eye and enquiring mind that is always present in human nature.

Striking similarities

On closer scrutiny, the creation stories of the Old Testament are not so dissimilar in their accounts of how the cosmos got started from the scientific knowledge at our disposal today. In the beginning, the universe was void and dark. Then came the first light, then the oceans, followed by the dry land. Then there appeared water-based creatures, followed by those which lived on dry land. Then at the end of a long, complex chain of biological development came Homo sapiens.

To my mind, the Big Bang Theory makes little difference to the belief that God created the universe and all that is within it. Creation and evolution are not incompatible but rather they are complimentary and together enable us to understand better the bigger picture. The evolution theory explains how the universe came into being, whereas the creation story gives the reason for its existence, as well as our own existence here on Earth.

I feel that Darwin has been misunderstood by many. As far as I know, he was not on an intentional quest to discredit the idea of the existence of God. He simply explained things according to his scientific observations. Darwin did lose his faith in God (whatever faith he already had, that is), but this was the result of losing his beloved daughter to illness, not so much his scientific theories (Nick Spencer, Darwin and God).

By way of aside, how do we cope with personal tragedy? If we have faith in God, it can be strengthened or weakened by these events. My wife and I suffered the loss of our first two children, first a girl and then, two years later, a boy. Following the first loss, we were counselled by one relative to abandon God, who was thought to be not much good to us. I replied that at that moment, we needed him more than ever, and that to abandon our faith would leave us with nothing as we struggled to get through those terrible days. We refused to abandon our faith and we did get through those most difficult days of our lives, because God spoke to us in ways we could not have imagined. Even in those darkest of times, he got through to us. We pursue this in more detail in our book, Encounters with God in Brazil: Personal stories to amaze and inspire, published by Kingdom Publishers.

But back to where we were. I have long held that creation and evolution can exist happily together and become the best of friends. Humans are still evolving as they always have, though my personal understanding is that they are different in origin from their fellow primates. And, I believe, there is a very good reason for saying this.

The jewel of creation

Human beings, according to the Bible, are made in the image of God. This is what makes us different from all other species, even the most advanced ones. This doesn't mean that other species are not created by God in fact the Bible says they are. It means they were not made to know God or to enjoy a relationship with him at a personal level. The creatures with whom we share planet Earth were made for our enjoyment and companionship and, also, because of the role they play in maintaining a balanced ecosystem. In different degrees, they have intelligence and share instincts with human beings, such as the instinct to survive, or to care for and protect their young. In fact, we share much of our DNA with all other living things from apes to bacteria.

That is also true of atoms from which all physical substances are formed, from individual human cells to planets and stars. We are all composed of atoms. Though atoms are different from one another in terms of their composition (depending on the number of protons in the nucleus), it is how these atoms are held together (which involves neutrons and electrons), that determines their essential character. That is whether the materials they form are shiny or dull, liquid or gas, hard or soft (see Keith Welch, Questions and Answers, Jefferson Lab Science Education).

For their part, molecules are made up of two or more atoms bonded together and are the basis of human cells. It is estimated that a human cell has in the region of 100 trillion atoms. So, we should not be surprised to learn that we share the same basic building blocks of life with everything around us, both living and inanimate.

In fact, we are not so very different from anything else in the universe. As Bishop Tom Wright says, "We all wear second-hand clothes in that respect" (New Heavens, New Earth, p.23). These are handed down to us as atoms that are recycled; they are used, dispensed with, and then re-appropriated for further use. We ourselves receive atoms from the food we eat, which are then reformulated into the molecules appropriate to our bodily needs. We began this book by saying: Nothing is new under the sun; talking of which, we are all basically stardust. We are all composed of the primordial material which is common to everything else. This has its origin in stars, the first objects to form and which gave rise to all other material.

This does not detract from our uniqueness in the world. No two people have the same fingerprints, and we are more than the sum of our biological parents. We all share the same basic building blocks of life at the molecular level. It is the specific arrangement of these molecules that is different from one person to another, and genetic variations and environmental influences all come into play to form the unique persons that we are.

The Bible tells us that primordial Man was formed from the dust of the ground as it is written in the Book of Genesis (2:7). How close to modern scientific thought and knowledge that is! But the Bible immediately adds something entirely significant to the beginnings of the story of Man when it says, "...and (the Lord God) breathed into his nostrils the breath of life; and man became a living being," It goes on to say:

> The Lord God planted a garden eastward in Eden, and there he put the man whom he had formed (Genesis 2:8).

It is clear from this that humans have something that is unique to creation apart from their evolved abilities to have dominion over the earth (Genesis 1:28).

There is an interesting article by a postdoctoral fellow of Stanford University who explained how humans evolved not from modern apes but from a common ancestor of both. The reason that apes continue to exist alongside humans was explained as the division of this species into two separate species due to environmental and evolutionary factors. One-half of this divide continued to live in the forest while the other half was forced to move out of the forest to open grasslands.

As a result, the latter had to learn to survive in different circumstances and developed the ability to walk upright and run further on two feet to escape predators and use the other two as hands to gather food and carry it home.

Although I find this argument interesting and fascinating, it seems to me that it may be a way of reasoning backwards to make the facts agree with an already established scientific theory. However, to be fair the author of this article does acknowledge that her explanation is based on a degree of probability, and on what might have happened, rather than scientific certainty.

Following on from the above article, it is true to say that humans share much of their DNA with apes. That is scientifically proven, so why deny it? Nevertheless, even with the basic acceptance of this premise, it seems to me self-evident that in many ways humans and apes are distinct species. In view of this, it is more accurate to say that humans are related to their fellow primates rather than that they evolved from them. And here we have two distinct concepts. We shall pursue this further in a moment.

There are two Bible texts that I should like to call upon at this point in our reflections. The first is from the Psalms:

> For you have formed my inward parts. You have covered me in my mother's womb. I will praise you, for I am fearfully and wonderfully made. Marvellous are your works, and that my soul knows very well. My frame was not hidden from you. When I was made in secret, and skilfully wrought in the lowest parts of the earth, your eyes saw my substance, being yet unformed. And in your book, they all were written. The days fashioned for me when as yet there were none of them (Psalm 139:13-16).

If we think carefully about these words, we may ask ourselves where they came from at such an early stage in human history. The psalmist seems to visualise his existence before he was formed but also that his existence was thought and willed by God. From where did we come if not from the primordial material to which we have referred? And how did we come to be as we are? Again, we have the answer from science. But these thoughts are not derived from science alone. These are *God thoughts* shared with the jewel of his creation, so that we humans might respond in gratitude to God and in recognition of our Maker. And we should, because we are known by him, encompassed by him, and the length of our days is determined by him. Artur Weiser sums up our inherent relationship to God when he says: "But it is not only the beginning of his life which is exposed to the clear light of God's knowledge; the total sum of the days he is permitted to live is also recorded by God in the *book of the living* and is therefore foreordained by the divine will even before these days actually come to pass" (The Psalms, p.806).

Interestingly, the idea that the number of our days is predetermined has entered the thought processes of people whether of a science or religious background or neither. It seems to be imprinted on our psyche and is perhaps a sign of our connectedness to the source of our being, even where no explicit recognition of God is present.

Why do things exist?

This is a question science cannot answer because it doesn't fall within the domain of science. But again, the Prologue of John's Gospel comes to mind:

> In the beginning was the Word, and the Word was with God, and the Word was God. He was in the beginning with God. All things were made through him, and without him nothing was made that was made (John 1:1-3).

Not only was humanity fashioned by God but also the entire universe. The above statements are statements of faith, but they have their basis in science, as well. Science can explain how the universe and everything in it was started, at least back to the point when time began, or the so-called Big Bang. But this is also the point at which physics breaks down and science can go no further.

To give an answer as to why the universe exists, science is still grasping at straws. Denis Alexander elaborates on this point when he says, "Many people think that when Christians talk about *creation* they are referring mainly to *origins*. Of course, the biblical teaching on creation includes origins, but if we become too focused on origins then we can forget that the biblical understanding of creation is not primarily concerned with how things began, but why they exist" (Creation or Evolution: Do we have to choose? p.27).

Where science can corroborate Scripture, it does. Where it cannot do this, we are left with Scripture alone to furnish the answers to our most pressing questions. Both science and Scripture say similar things about the formation of the universe and human life but use different language in doing so. Where science resorts to the existence of an impersonal, mysterious force behind the Big Bang, this the Bible explains as God. In this respect, there is a similar relationship between Greek and Hebrew thought as G. Campbell Morgan points out in the following:

The Hebrew philosopher said, "Things postulate thought. Wherever there is a thing, it proves a thought. The thing is the outcome of the thought. If things postulate thought, thought postulates a thinker." The Greek philosopher did not go so far as that. The Greek philosopher said: "Behind all things there must be thought, but the thought is abstract." The Hebrew philosopher said, "You cannot have an abstract thought unless you have a thinker" (Studies in the Four Gospels: The Gospel According to John, p.21).

If we look again at the story in Genesis, we will see that on the first day God created light; on the second day he created the sky, and on the third day, the earth. If we follow the scientific sequence of events here, there appears to be little difference between the two versions of events. Of course, day and night are not of the same duration in each account, but it is interesting that day follows night in both, giving rise to the *first morning*. The difference in the scientific view, like that of the Greek philosopher, is that the work of creation is seen as the result of impersonal forces. However, if we follow the line of the Hebrew philosopher, we only need to look in a mirror to see the reflection of a person. And persons, according to Hebrew thought, do not appear from nowhere. They are the product of previous thought, which is personal in origin and the origin of personhood, the essential characteristic of all human beings.

Morgan also helpfully explains that in the above reference to John's Gospel, the word *was*, in the original Greek is used in every instance in the imperfect tense, giving the impression of continuity or timelessness. This should resolve a question that science is presently divided about; that is whether the universe has a beginning. Scripture allows us a shot at the answer. The universe did have a beginning, but God does not. Or to put this in scientific language: *the mysterious force* behind the Big Bang existed before time, but the Big Bang is the point at which time began.

This is all very fascinating from both a scientific and theological point of view because, to my mind, the one answers the question the other is asking. And that does not mean that one is wrong, and the other is right. In fact, both are right and when we view them together, we get an answer as to the exact origin of the universe.

In the unfolding of John's thought, he proceeds to say, "without him nothing was made that was made" (1:3). This references the whole of creation and includes us. Coming at the beginning of John's Gospel, it resonates with and echoes the first chapter of the Book of Genesis. What does it mean that we are made in the image of God? What has that to say about the structure of personhood? I agree with those Bible analysts who say that every human being is essentially a single integrated entity consisting of body, soul, and spirit. Though distinguishable, these three dimensions of our being are not to be considered as separate compartments within personhood but are each an integral part of the whole.

Denis Alexander seems to be making a similar point when he says that in the context of the Hebrew creation stories, Adam's soul (*nephesh*) represents his status as a living being and is not to be understood as something added on or separate from what he became, when God breathed into his nostrils the breath of life (Creation or Evolution, pp.194-95).

Let us look at it this way; on the one hand, the soul and spirit are as much a part of me as the body. On the other hand, our redemption includes the body as well as the soul and spirit. The fact is our material body is changed many times over in a lifetime. It is not physically the same body with which we are born. The aging process would indicate this, as the body's cells are constantly being replaced but not reproduced exactly as before. So our true self is clearly more than the physical body. The body can, therefore, be likened to an outward garment, which we dispose of when we die. Having said that, our body, soul and spirit are all present in the glorious resurrection self to which we aspire, and for which we long. I am speaking from a Christian point of view and should clarify that this last sentiment may not be shared by all, for one reason or another.

But then, deep down in our innermost being, is there not a desire for God insofar as that which gives ultimate purpose and meaning to life? Many good people are bold enough to dismiss God from their lives when life is good and sometimes otherwise. However, at life's end there is often a marked degree of despair felt by those for whom that God-shaped space within has not been filled with his light and love, leading to other questions for which there is no answer.

Where thoughts of God do exist also raises the question as to where they came from. That is unless we live in a closed world to all that is going on around us and even to our own existence and what that means. Homo sapiens are not only intelligent beings but also thinking beings with an awareness of themselves, as well as time and eternity. When all these wonderful facets of human life are put together, it would be difficult to deny that the major existential questions are not naturally among the most seriously contemplated by human beings.

Returning to my original point, I do not consider the body to be intrinsically evil or to be shunned, as in Greek Gnostic teaching, which also rejects the humanity of Christ for the very reason that God could never assume human form. The soul as an integral part of personhood is generally understood to be the seat of our real self, our consciousness, feelings, and emotions. It is what makes us tick humanly speaking. There would appear to be more to us than a complex series of non-personal chemical processes in the brain. Apart from our cognitive ability to find solutions that facilitate our day-to-day lives, which is also evident in other living species, there is the human awareness or consciousness of right and wrong or the knowledge of good and evil referred to in the Genesis story of creation (2:9b, 16-17). But it is God's Spirit (Hb. ruach, Gk. pneuma), which God breathed into the first human being, that essentially distinguishes us from the rest of the animal kingdom. The basis for our understanding here is found in the following:

> And the Lord God formed man of the dust of the ground, and breathed into his nostrils the breath of life, and man became a living being (Genesis 2:7).

It is this important difference that sets us apart from all other earthly species. This also plays out in our continuing relationship with God. God is spirit and those who worship him do so *in spirit and in truth* (John 4:23-24). This is worship that involves both the heart and mind and is focused on God and who he is. According to the Bible, it is in the context of their relationship to God that humans are different from the rest of the created order.

In another, but complimentary version of the creation story we read:

> Then God said, "Let us make man in our image, according to our likeness..." So God created man in his own image, in the image of God he created him; male and female he created them (Genesis 1:26-27).

Because of this intrinsic difference, unique to humans, we can know God and seek after him, which he invites us to do (Isaiah 55:6).

Returning to a matter raised earlier in this book, there is a philosophical trend that accepts the existence of God but considers that having set everything in motion he withdrew from his work of creation. This is one way of answering some of the fundamental questions about God. This kind of reasoning allows for the existence of God but argues that he is remote and indifferent to the world. This line of philosophical thought is known as Deism. Perhaps the question most often asked is, if there is a God why is there so much suffering in the world? The implication here is that there is no God. This is a very difficult question to answer. But God's unfolding purposes as revealed in the Bible give us the clue as we seek to respond to this kind of question.

The classic treatise on undeserved suffering in the Bible is found in the Book of Job. At the end of this book when Job challenges God about his tragic situation in life, God doesn't respond with an explanation for Job's troubles. Rather he invites Job to consider the wonders of creation and to know that God is God. It is an invitation to trust God in all things, and in all the circumstances of life. God doesn't always do things the way we expect or want. But he is there for us all the time, and in every circumstance. At the very heart of this is the cross.

Denis Alexander makes an important point when he says, "Christ on the cross provided an answer to death and suffering, not a reason for it" (Science and Christianity, p.162). For this, we can draw on the fact that this world is by no means perfect, not that it was created as such, in fact far from it. The world is a fallen world waiting for its redemption together with the children of God. This is in preparation and anticipation of a glorious future when his reign is firmly established in the hearts of men and women. God created us human beings to enjoy fellowship with himself, in a living, meaningful, and purposeful relationship. This is true of all human beings even for those who are unaware of the potential relationship that they have with God.

To respond to the idea that God has set the world in motion and left it to its own devices is not particularly satisfactory. Because when things are left to look after themselves, they tend to function less well, or break down, as in the analogy of the watch and the watchmaker, to which we referred earlier.

That does not seem to be the case with the universe. Stars come and go. They die, but others are born. The universe continues to grow; it is not static. The world continues to evolve. Moreover, humans can and do relate to God, and he does intervene in human affairs and situations. These interventions are often rationalised or dismissed as coincidence, but I would posit that God does sustain his creation and has not withdrawn either from the physical universe or from the realm of human affairs. As a sign of the relationship, we have with him, he sends us into the world to make him known by word and deed, in every city, town and village of our global community.

For further personal reflection or group discussion:

How may we reconcile the Genesis story with modern scientific facts about creation?

What are the benefits of science and faith working together for a better understanding of the universe?

Has personal tragedy strengthened or weakened your faith in God?

If we are made from material common to everything that exists, how are we as humans different from all other living things?

How would you respond to someone who says, "If there is a God, he is no longer involved in the workings of the universe"?

CHAPTER THREE
A NEW EARTH AND A NEW HEAVEN

The Bible, in both the Old and New Testaments, refers to a new heaven and a new earth. But how different will these be from the existing heaven and earth? We are informed by astrophysicists that the present earth will eventually become engulfed by the sun as its fuel is exhausted and it expands into a red giant, before retracting to a white dwarf. By then the earth will be no more than a scorched cinder and life will have ceased to exist throughout the solar system.

We are talking in terms of billions of years into the future, far beyond our lifetimes, but inexorably that day will come. The words of the Apostle Peter support this foreboding scenario in the context of the long-anticipated return of Jesus as ruler of heaven and earth.

> The heavens, being on fire, will be dissolved, and the elements will melt with fervent heat (2 Peter 3:12).

It is unlikely that Peter had in mind a time span of billions of years into the future, but the tone is a prophetic one, nonetheless, and confirmed in the following:

> Nevertheless, we, according to his promise, look for new heavens and a new earth in which righteousness dwells (2 Peter 3:13).

Here Peter treads the familiar path of a long-held expectation that the existing heavens (the skies and celestial bodies) will pass away, and a new order will be established on Earth. This expectation on the part of God's people is taken to new levels of descriptive detail by the Apostle John in the Book of Revelation.

How new is new?

As we begin to assimilate the implications of this cataclysmic event, are we to understand from John's vision that th*is new* earth will be totally new, different, or other (Gk. *Kaine*), one that will completely replace the existing earth and heavens? Or does it carry the more restricted meaning of *renewed (neos)*? In a similar vein, the Apostle Paul declares that those who are in Christ are a *new creation* (2 Corinthians 5:17).

Following his use here of *kaine*, which means *different*, in the sense of *other*, compared to the previous old version, it is of importance to note that in the Old and New Testaments, God does not discard the old or imperfect. Rather, he takes it and refashions it for his glory.

If we remember the prophet Jeremiah and the potter's wheel, we will know that God does not discard the marred vessel. Instead, he takes it again and reworks it into something aesthetically pleasing and fit for purpose (Jeremiah 18.1-4). This also works out in the context of daily life. Following his emphatic denial of Jesus, Peter is restored as the leader of the pack and reinstated as the pastor of God's church (John 21:15-17).

Peter is an excellent example of what it means to be clay in the potter's hands. When we become malleable for God and place ourselves in his hands, this always serves our best interests and is a unique opportunity to have our broken lives mended for God's glory. The same goes for our broken world, a world for which Jesus died on a Roman cross. God has pledged himself to make good of this world and of this earth, according to his promise passed down through the generations of his people.

Ruth Valerio, in <u>Saying Yes to Life</u>, supports this view as follows: "When you became a Christian you didn't become a totally new human being... such a use of *new* carries with it both continuity and discontinuity," (pp.102-103).

With this, she also draws attention to Bishop Tom Wright "who has long argued against the view that our eternal future is in a non-physical heaven" (<u>New Heavens and New Earth: The biblical picture of Christian hope</u>).

Then with reference to David Wilkinson's <u>Christian Eschatology</u>, Valerio also asserts, "our final destiny is on the united and transformed heaven on Earth, within a transformed universe."

Where is heaven?

Returning to the Old Testament, in Psalm 19, the psalmist writes eloquently about heaven and earth: "The heavens declare the glory of God; and the firmament shows his handiwork" (Psalm 19:1).

Hebrew poetry characteristically employs parallelisms, where an idea is repeated using different words. In this example, the word for '*heavens*' in the first part of the verse, is rendered '*sky*' in the second part. This would suggest that for the psalmist heaven and sky are practically one and the same, because here he is referring to the celestial bodies we observe above and around us. However, we can be equally sure that heaven, as in *God's abode*, is not up in the sky. For instance, when Jesus ascended to heaven, he did not go *up*. That is simply a human spatial concept reflecting the way we see the world and its relationship to the cosmos, and, as this was understood in the Ancient Near East. The vacuum of space is '*out there*' not '*up there*'. I am not trying to score points with this, only to reflect on the way we sometimes understand the world and its place and setting in the universe.

Even if heaven were somewhere in the sky, it is not *up there*. It is more correct to say that it's *out* there or all around us. But even this way of articulating the way we perceive the heavens is erroneously two-dimensional. The universe is, of course, three-dimensional, or even four-dimensional if one allows for Einstein's space-time dimension.

Let us go on a journey, a journey further than you've ever undertaken before. For a moment, try and place yourself in the depths of outer space, far beyond the earth. The heavens would be all around you, above you and, strangely, as never before, below you. You would find yourself floating and weightless, and seeing the cosmos, as it really is, in true 3D, above, below, and around you, without end, in all directions, whichever way you looked. And it would not be science fiction, but science fact. To say the least, the experience would give you a weird, never-before experienced, sinking feeling in the pit of the stomach.

The words of Christina Rossetti's classic poem, turned Christmas carol, come to mind at this point. In this, she contemplates the dramatically unequal relationship between heaven and earth and their creator God:

> Our God, heaven cannot hold him, nor earth sustain,
> heaven and earth shall flee away when he comes to reign.

If we pause for a moment and think about this, then the Creator, or *cause*, of the universe must necessarily be greater than his creation, and his presence, power and authority will also be greater than the capacity of the universe to contain him. Yet, it is truly remarkable that of all the planets in the universe, large and small, far, and relatively near, in astronomical terms, ours is the only one where human life is known to exist. I would suggest that this is far more extraordinary than the existence of all the stars and planets, and their respective moons put together.

Paula Gooder draws our attention to the interesting fact that in the Bible the heavens and the earth are bound together from their creation to their dissolution. They will both cease to exist in their present form, and both will be made new. Heaven will not last forever any more than the earth (Where on Earth is Heaven? p.7).

Jesus makes this point, when he declares that even though heaven and earth will pass away, God's word will remain until it is entirely fulfilled (Matthew 5.18). Gooder makes the following insightful observation in her book: "It is easy to assume that heaven is far away... but the biblical tradition suggests that heaven... though veiled from earth, is very close to it" (Ibid. p.8). There is a connectedness between the two and they share a mutual destiny.

The Apostle Paul, addressing the Greek philosophers in Athens, declares:

> For in him we live and move and have our being (Acts 17:28).

Yes, God is not far from us, but Paul takes this a step further when he declares that we are the temple of the Holy Spirit, the dwelling place of God.

> Do you not know that you are the temple of God and that the Spirit of God dwells in you? (1 Corinthians 3.16; see also 6:19-20).

If we take these two Pauline statements together, we arrive at the conclusion that God is around us and within us.

This is not a refinement of Pantheism where God is everything and in everything. In making these affirmations, we are contemplating the work of the triune God, Father, Son, and Holy Spirit. Though God reveals himself to us as three persons, they work in harmony as one; each fulfilling and completing God's work on Earth, through his people. It is important that here we should again make the distinction between heaven as *sky* and heaven *where God is*. This, of course, does not detract in any way from the reality that God is omnipresent or everywhere.

Cosmic happenings

In making his statements about the immanence of God (the immediacy of his presence), Paul also leans on his well-grounded understanding of the Hebrew Scriptures. In so doing, he recalls the words of the prophet Isaiah:

> Do not remember the former things nor consider the things of old. Behold, I will do a new thing. Now it shall spring forth; shall you not know it? I will even make a road in the wilderness and rivers in the desert (Isaiah 43:18-19).

This sits well with other eschatological events (those related to the end times) such as the future millennium when, according to the

Apostle John's vision, Christ will return and reign on Earth with the saints for a thousand years. Moreover, Paul's anticipation of the rapture, when we shall be taken up to meet him in the air, in no way conflicts with Christ's rule on Earth. Patrick Miller, in his blog, observes that the rapture is a throwback to a tradition when the people went out from the city to meet the returning emperor after a period away, and then to form a procession for the purpose of accompanying him into the city of Rome.

As Miller says: "Crowds would leave the city to meet the king outside the gates, and then usher him back in. This same thing happened when Jesus entered Jerusalem on Palm Sunday, when the crowds went out to meet him and usher him into the city" (Is the Rapture Real? The Crossing). Paul, the Apostle, in similar fashion, would have been accompanied by the Christians who lived in Rome on the final stage of his long-awaited journey, in chains, to that imperial city.

In the Book of Revelation, the Apostle John, while living in exile on the island of Patmos, has a vision of a new heaven and earth.

> And I saw a new heaven and a new earth: for the first heaven and the first earth had passed away (Revelation 21:1).

The central feature of this eschatological reality is the New Jerusalem coming down from heaven to earth.

> Then I, John saw the holy city, New Jerusalem, coming down out of heaven from God, prepared as a bride adorned for her husband (Revelation 21:2).

It is worth noting here, that some thirty-five years before the Book of Revelation was written, the Apostle Paul alludes to the church as the bride of Christ. This he does in his letter to the Ephesians (Chapter 5). With these, we can see that the nature of the celestial city as a gathered community takes precedence over the concept of a material building. This redeemed community belongs to Christ and is the object of his love, and the reason for his sacrificial death on the cross (5:25).

The bride, who will descend from heaven, is the personification of the glory of the church, beautifully adorned and ready to meet her husband. The notion of a celestial city is symbolic of a reality otherwise beyond description. The fact that the New Jerusalem will come down from heaven to earth appears to confirm that this earth will be the centre and sphere of God's future, heavenly rule.

In his exegesis of the same passage of Scripture, George Beasley-Murray makes this observation: "The city has the extraordinary function of uniting earth and heaven" (New Bible Commentary Revised, p.1308).

Heaven and earth are two separate realities, and both are made new in the purposes of God. They share a mutual destiny insofar as they will be joined and become one, as a bride and her husband.

Paula Gooder also makes this same point when she says: "the new heaven and earth will be united and no longer seemingly separate" (Where on Earth is Heaven? p.35). Furthermore, N.T. Wright maintains, "the great claim of Revelation 21 and 22 is that heaven and earth will finally be united" (New Heavens, New Earth, p.11).

It is evident that there are many respected voices articulating these same thoughts and ideas, as they seek to interpret God's Word faithfully. Demonstrably, these insights are not based on the interpretation of isolated thinkers, a few forward-thinking people swimming against the tide of mainstream theology. Together, they form a growing consensus that, in God's purposes, heaven and earth will become one at the consummation of the age.

The wider context to this is found in the following verses:

> And I heard a loud voice from heaven saying, "Behold, the tabernacle of God is with men, and he will dwell with them, and they shall be his people, and God himself will be with them, and be their God. And God will wipe away every tear from their eyes; there shall be no more death, nor sorrow, nor crying, and there shall be no more pain, for the former things have passed away." Then he who sat on the throne said, "Behold, I make all things new." And he said to me, "Write, for these words are true and faithful." And he said unto me, "It is done! I am the Alpha and Omega, the Beginning, and the End. I will give of the water of the fountain of life freely to him who thirsts. He who overcomes shall inherit all things, and I will be his God, and he shall be my son" (Revelation 21:3-7).

The concept of the tabernacle of God is reminiscent of the Fourth Gospel, written by the same author. Here the sense is of God *making his dwelling* or literally pitching his tent among humankind on the earth:

> And the Word became flesh, and dwelt among us, and we beheld his glory, the glory as of the only begotten of the Father, full of grace and truth (John 1:14).

This last passage reflects the importance that John attaches to the incarnation and what this decisive event in human history has to do with us. As we say elsewhere in this book, where Jesus is, there also is heaven, because Jesus is the incarnate presence of God on Earth.

Returning to the idea of a united heaven and earth, we come to a phrase in Revelation 21:5, Behold, I make all things new *kaina panta*. This has the sense of brand new or *radically* new, but in the wider context of this passage and Scripture as a whole, could naturally involve the concept of taking something old and transforming it into something quite different from its previous state. Sadness is transformed into joy, tears into laughter, death into life. The *former things* are no longer.

From the basis of the old, something new has taken their place, and necessarily so. With the purpose of underlining this point, I refer to George Beasley-Murray who cites the inadequacy of "the present creation, at least in its present form, to be the scene of the perfected eternal kingdom of God" (New Bible Commentary Revised, p.1307).

In the context of a united heaven and earth, the declaration by Jesus, He who overcomes shall inherit all things (Revelation 21:7), is also akin to his declaration concerning the meek in the Sermon on the Mount (Matthew 5:5). In his message to the gathered multitude, Jesus was clearly referring to planet Earth. Is it not stretching things too far to assume that the earth was in God's sights here, too?

This declaration by Jesus made within the context of the Beatitudes would suggest a new world order is to be inaugurated when he comes again to earth. But, also, to the new earth where justice and peace will prevail together with a right and fair distribution of the earth's resources. We can note here that it is the meek who will become the stewards of this new order, which is those who act not out of self-interest but for the good of all, in which all will share in the benefits and rewards of God's *new* earth and its production.

In the Bible and Jesus' own use of this word, meek means humble, gentle, and patient, of inner strength, resilience, and self-control. Therefore, its meaning here is quite different from the modern understanding of a weak and submissive person who is easily manipulated (see Richard Glover, The Gospel of Matthew, pp.41-42).

Return to Eden

Lastly, I would draw your attention to Paul's allusion to the entire creation that is awaiting the revealing of the children of God for its own liberation from the downward, gravitational pull of corruption and sin (Romans 8:19). When this happens, the world will be as we imagine heaven to be, insofar as all creation will coexist in peace and harmony, as foretold by the Old Testament prophet Isaiah in the following superb description of this new world and its inhabitants.

> They shall beat their swords into ploughshares, and their spears into pruning-hooks. Nation shall not lift sword against nation, neither shall they learn war anymore (Isaiah 2:4).

The vision of a future perfect world is described not only in terms of human relations, but also in terms of its kindly impact on the animal kingdom:

> The wolf also shall dwell with the lamb. The leopard shall lie down with the young goat. The calf and the young lion and the fatling together and a little child shall lead them (Isaiah 11:6).

Unless this is to be understood as purely symbolic language, what Isaiah has in view is the present world order renewed and transformed. That would also appear to include the present earth as an integral part of God's creation, which waits for the day of its redemption. An important element of biblical hermeneutics, or the science of interpretation, is to recognise the way language is used, whether literally or symbolically, or in some other way such as allegory or hyperbole. Measurements and numbers often have a symbolic value in Scripture, as in the description of the size of the heavenly Jerusalem.

Another example is the number 40. It is quite reasonable to take this value literally, wherever it arises in the Bible, but it also has symbolic value and has to do with a sufficient time or completeness. Multiples of 12 are another example of the use of numerical symbolism in the Bible. My own view is to go with the most natural interpretation of a passage or text rather than force it into one category or another. So, for this reason, I would regard Isaiah's description of a future world as a concrete example of how the new reality will pan out. This represents a return to the way things were when man was given dominion over the primordial garden.

> Then God blessed them, and God said to them, "Be fruitful and multiply; fill the earth and subdue it; have dominion over the fish of the sea, over the birds of the air, and over every living thing that moves on the earth" (Genesis 1:28).

This, I believe, is also true of Paul's declaration when writing to the church in Rome:

> Because the creation itself also will be delivered from the bondage of corruption into the glorious liberty of the children of God (Romans 8:21).

Just as humanity awaits its redemption in due course, so does God's entire work of creation. Both are bound together in the consequences and possibilities of their present and future states respectively.

F.F. Bruce explains this point, as follows: "It is not only Christians who have this hope of glory. All creation is waiting with earnest longing for the day when the sons of God will be manifested in glory" (The Epistle of Paul to the Romans, pp.168-69).

Does this mean that one day we will return to the Garden of Eden or something like it? The answer, I think, is *yes* and *no*. The world, as God intended it to be, will be restored. God is still the master of his creation. Humankind, driven by economics and the concentration of wealth and power in the hands of the few has distorted the earth. God has given us the ability to choose, an essential part of what it means to be human. But however perfectly we are made, apparent flaws have emerged in our makeup.

The primordial story acknowledges one of these flaws where our freedom to choose was used as an opportunity to do the right thing by us and not what was ordained by God. So does this mean that our freedom to choose is a flawed asset? Perhaps not as we would be less than fully human without this *flaw*. Whatever the answer to this conundrum, the situation has led to a distortion of the planet which was originally intended to be for the benefit of all the world's inhabitants, fauna and flora included.

We can note here at this point in our reflection, that the concept of a paradisal garden bears a resemblance, a parallel, to our once rural-based societies. But then the movement of the world's population from rural communities towards the cities and the reality of modern-day living seems to have its own parallel in the biblical stories of the garden and the city. This is reflected in the new heaven and earth set out before us in the vision of John the apostle toward the close of his life and the close of the Bible, also. And as it closes, the Bible appears to point beyond itself to a day when the new city dwellers will live by the word of God, as the prophet had said they would, one day (Jeremiah 31:33).

As far as it is possible to give a timeline to these events, this glorious future will begin with the inauguration of the millennial reign of Christ. This, itself, is of limited duration and will be followed by the appearance of the new heaven and earth. After this, the Holy City, also known as the Bride of Christ, will come down from heaven to earth. However, between now and then, there will be all kinds of happenings and troubles from natural disasters to the destruction we bring upon ourselves. Destruction generated by fear, suspicion, and greed that inevitably leads to war, including the mother of all battles – Armageddon.

There are signs that this is already shaping up, possibly on a global scale, with serious rumblings in the Middle East. If you wish to know when the final battle will come to pass, then look to the land of Israel, which is exactly where this final battle will take place.

Here already, but not yet

With the birth of Christ, the end times have drawn significantly closer. At the outset of his earthly ministry, Jesus announced that the kingdom of God had arrived.

> Now after John was put in prison, Jesus came to Galilee, preaching the gospel of the kingdom of God, and saying, "The time is fulfilled, and the kingdom of

> God is at hand. Repent, and believe in the gospel" (Mark 1:14-15).

And this kingdom was indeed present in the person of Jesus, himself, a reality demonstrated both in the authority with which he spoke and the nature of his works, the evidence that God was at work among the people.

Matthew also records these words of Jesus regarding the nearness of God's kingdom:

> From that time Jesus began to preach and to say, "Repent, for the kingdom of heaven is at hand" (Matthew 4:17).

Mark was, of course, writing with a Roman audience in mind, whilst Matthew's Gospel was directed to the Jewish community. There is no essential difference in the meaning of *kingdom of heaven* and *kingdom of God* in these two accounts. This simply reflects the writer's reticence in referring to God directly by name on the part of Matthew and in deference to his Jewish readers. But it does bring us to consider the tension between the *now* and the *yet to be* aspects of God's kingly rule on Earth. A leading exponent of the idea that God's kingdom has come in the person and ministry of Jesus is Professor C. H. Dodd, who coined the term *Realised Eschatology*. I would concur that the reign of God on Earth has begun, but it is also yet to be in respect of its final consummation.

In some theological circles, the present time, often referred to as the Age of the Church, is also thought to equate with the millennium or one-thousand-year rule of Christ on Earth. Those who hold this view believe that Christ will return at the close of this thousand-year period described in the Book of Revelation. So according to this view, the millennium is already in progress.

On the other hand, there are those who expect Christ to return first, before inaugurating his reign of a thousand years. Both groups are biblical in their beliefs about Christ's redemptive work on the cross but share different views regarding the end times. The difference is a matter of chronology, of *when* not *if*.

In the last week of his earthly ministry, Jesus challenged the Jewish authorities regarding the destruction and rebuilding of the temple in Jerusalem. By way of his reference to a three-day timescale for this to happen, we understand that he was referring to his own death and resurrection. For centuries, the temple was the traditional dwelling place of God on Earth. From then on, Jesus had replaced the temple as the expression of God's presence among his people. This was symbolically shown to be true with the rending of the veil in the temple at the hour Jesus gave his dying breath on the cross. Significantly, the veil was torn from top to bottom, signifying that this was an action from above on God's part.

That Jesus was to be the new meeting-place between God and man was announced to Joseph, Mary's betrothed, by the angel Gabriel:

> Behold, a virgin shall be with child, and bear a son, and
> they shall call his name Immanuel, which is translated,
> God with us (Matthew 1:23).

This new meeting-place is no longer restricted to a single locality as was the temple built with human hands over a period of forty years, neither that temple nor the previous one built by King Solomon.

Solomon was perfectly aware of the inadequacy of a temple built by human hands (I Kings 8:27). Jesus replaced the temple and is also the mediator, representing God to man and man to God:

> For there is one God, and one mediator between God and men, the man Christ Jesus (1 Timothy 2:5).

What is more, his *once and for all* sacrifice on the cross replaced the necessity of repeated sacrifices in the Jerusalem Temple (Hebrews 7:25-27). In Jesus, both the temple and its sacrifices have become obsolete.

The kingdom or rule of God on Earth is already at hand. This is evidenced by the miracles performed by Jesus in biblical times to our own day. They are signs of God's powerful activity among us and there is more to come. The Apostle John was privileged to get a glimpse of this, through the curtain of heaven:

> Then I saw an angel coming down from heaven, having the key to the bottomless pit and a great chain in his hand. He laid hold of the dragon, that serpent of old, who is the Devil and Satan, and bound him for a thousand years; and he cast him into the bottomless pit, and shut him up, and set a seal on him, so that he should deceive the nations no more, till the thousand years were finished. But after these things, he must be released for a little while. And I saw thrones and they (those who were slain) sat on them, and judgment was committed to them. And I saw the souls of those who had been beheaded for their witness to Jesus and for the word of God, who had not worshiped the beast or his image, and had not received his mark on their foreheads or on their hands. And they lived and reigned with Christ for a thousand years. But the rest of the dead did not live again until the thousand years were

finished. This is the first resurrection. Blessed and holy is he who has part in the first resurrection. Over such the second death has no power, but they shall be priests of God and of Christ and shall reign with him a thousand years (Revelation 20:1-6).

In the Sermon on the Mount, Jesus says the meek will inherit the earth, apparently in a future sense (Matthew 5.5). Nevertheless, the present and future reality of the kingdom of God suggests that this beatitude also has a subordinate present meaning. Here the meek are implicitly urged to make a difference to earthly situations now, in anticipation of the full realisation of God's kingdom on Earth.

In the Book of Revelation, where past and future interpretations of events are both possible, the future is brought into special focus with the arrival on Earth of the heavenly Jerusalem (Revelation 21:9-10). The apostle's vision, in which he sees future events as they unfold, is of a future to be enacted here on Earth at the close of the present age. There is every reason, therefore, to believe that our home planet will feature prominently in God's plans for a new heaven and earth.

When the lights go out

Cosmologists and astrophysicists, those who specialise in the study of the universe, tell us that stars do not last forever. One day they will burn themselves out, as many already have or are in the process of doing so. Betelgeuse, in the constellation of Orion, clearly visible from Earth, is an example of this happening right now. In so doing, such stars expand enormously and become red giants. Our local star, the sun, will suffer this same fate in about six billion years. As a result, it will engulf the earth and other planets of the inner solar system, possibly Mars, as well.

So where does this leave Earth in the long-term? The Bible tells us that the earth will be destroyed by fire, together with all the stars. Of course, stars are balls of incandescent gas so will burn themselves out rather than burn up. To counter this, the Book of Revelation explains that in the heavenly city, the New Jerusalem, God, himself, will be our sun and light:

> And the city had no need of the sun or of the moon to shine in it, for the glory of God illuminated it, and the Lamb is its light. And there shall be no night there: They need no lamp nor light of the sun, for the Lord God gives them light. And they shall reign forever and ever (Revelation 21:23; 22:5).

In the revelation of Jesus Christ to John, the apostle, foresees the demise of the sun and Earth, in fact, the whole universe, as we know it. So this is not overlooked but included in the grand scheme of things from a biblical point of view. Is heaven, therefore, to be found within the universe or is heaven a parallel state not affected by these forebodings? Well, indeed, it is included in these forebodings, and very much so. The present earth will be transformed beyond recognition amid these catastrophic cosmic events. This earth will not be dissolved before the coming of Christ, but the Bible indicates that these things will happen when he comes. Peter alludes to these things, so that we are not overtaken by surprise, though many will be taken unawares, those who are unprepared. Because Christ will return like a thief in the night when their guard is down:

> But the day of the Lord will come as a thief in the night, in which the heavens will pass away with a great noise, and the elements will melt with fervent heat; both the earth and the works that are in it will be burned up (2 Peter 3:10).

To maintain the integrity of the text, this verse needs to be reconciled with the thousand-year rule of Christ on Earth. The destruction spoken of here refers to the consequences to be faced by the false teachers who attempt to turn the faithful away from the word of truth, especially regarding the return of Christ. In the NIV, this verse ends with the words "the elements will be destroyed by fire, and the earth and everything done in it will be laid bare." This also runs parallel to the gospel teaching regarding the wheat and the chaff:

> His winnowing fan is in his hand, and he will thoroughly purge his threshing-floor and gather the wheat into his barn; but the chaff he will burn with unquenchable fire (Luke 3.17; see also Matthew 3:12).

This may not fully answer the question regarding the physical destruction of the earth by our dying local star, the sun. There is, however, a degree of uncertainty among scientists as to the number of planets that will be engulfed by our sun at its demise. Mercury and Venus, which are closest to the sun, are certain candidates, though there is less certainty as to whether Earth will be overtaken by such a fate. The earth is slowly moving away from the sun as the sun's gravitational pull on our planet lessens over time. Is this God's provision for planet Earth?

The prospect of the eventual demise of the sun and survival of the earth corresponds to the narrative in the Book of Revelation. As we have seen, the Bible affirms that Christ will be our light and sun and we will reign with him forever and ever. This is what we know, and of this, we can be certain. What we do not have the answers for, we must leave in the domain of the Creator of heaven and earth.

In 1772, John Newton wrote the words of what was to become the well-loved hymn, *'Amazing Grace'*. The last two verses of this hymn resonate perfectly with the setting we have contemplated:

The earth shall soon dissolve like snow,
The sun forbear to shine;
But God, who called me here below,
Will be forever mine.
When we've been there ten thousand years,
Bright shining as the sun,
We've no less days to sing God's praise
Than when we'd first begun.

These inspired words also give us another view of what it means to live eternally in God's presence. It is not so much that time does not end; rather that time is not used up. In eternity, we will always have the same amount of time before us, whatever amount of time we have already spent there or has already passed. In other words, we will find ourselves in a *timeless world* where time passes but is not actually spent. This is not the whole story, as far as eternity is concerned, but I do find the words of Newton's hymn a helpful way of describing one aspect of our multi-faceted life beyond the end times.

For further personal reflection or group discussion:

How does God deal with us when things go wrong in our lives?

How can we adapt our language to modern ways of thinking about heaven?

What analogy does the Bible use to describe the future union of heaven and earth? Do you find this analogy helpful? Give a reason for your response.

Can scientific predictions regarding planet earth be reconciled with the biblical vision of a renewed heaven and earth?

What can we learn about eternity from John Newton's hymn, Amazing Grace?

CHAPTER FOUR
BEYOND PARADISE

Heaven and Paradise are two words often used synonymously. The Garden of Eden is a translation of the proper noun *Paradise,* which comes from terminology that originated in ancient Persia and means a *walled garden.* (The New Bible Dictionary, p.934).

Jesus said to the dying thief on the cross that he would that same day be with him in Paradise. This does not mean the full realisation of heaven, but importantly, of being with Jesus or in the presence of Jesus. Though death separates us from loved ones it cannot separate us from the love of God (Romans 8:38-39).

Humans were expelled from the paradisal Garden of Eden at the beginning of their existence on Earth. In post-exilic Jewish thought, Paradise was the abode of the godly departed and referred as much to a state of being as to a physical place. Today, it is commonplace for us to refer to a person as being in a *'good place'* or otherwise regarding their mental, emotional, or spiritual well-being. The shift from belief in the abode of the dead as being a silent, shadowy, and non-descript existence (Hb. Sheol) to a place of rest and reward for the godly righteous, came about because of Israel's contact with Persian religious ideas during the exile in Babylonia.

While the biblical creation story stands in contrast to other creation stories elsewhere in the Ancient Near East, the Persian idea of Paradise is one that served to refine Jewish thinking about death and the departed. It also serves as an illustration of God's progressive revelation of his purposes for Israel from the call of Abraham to the death and resurrection of Jesus.

Touching heaven

To take this further, the Apostle Paul gives us to understand that Paradise and heaven are to all intents and purposes one and the same. He seems to be making this point when he attempts to describe what is frankly, an indescribable experience that he once had:

> I know a man in Christ who fourteen years ago – whether in the body I do not know, or whether out of the body I do not know, God knows – such a one was caught up to the third heaven. And I know such a man – whether in the body or out of the body I do not know, God knows – how he was caught up into Paradise and heard inexpressible words, which it is not lawful for a man to utter (2 Corinthians 12:2-4).

When we consider Paul's experience of heaven and John's vision of the new heaven, we are inexorably drawn to the conclusion that heaven, as it is now, and the new heaven, as it will be, are not one and the same reality.

Robert Haldane makes am interesting observation when he says: "This indeed cannot mean that the plants and animals as they at present exist shall be restored; but that the condition of those things which shall belong to the new heavens and the new earth, prepared for the sons of God shall be delivered from the curse, and restored to a perfect state, as when all things that God had created were pronounced by Him *very good*, and when, as at the beginning, before sin entered, they shall be fully adapted to the use of man" (The Epistle to the Romans, p.370).

This is a rear-view image of Isaiah's prophecy about the wolf and lamb, to which we referred in the previous chapter. The original characters are preserved but in a totally different world. In the same way this present earth will feature in the future version, as indeed do we ourselves; perfectly recognisable for who we are, and indeed were, but adapted to the new earth, anticipated by the present earth with eager longing. This new and future reality is also, not surprisingly, mirrored in Jesus' resurrection body, unmistakeably the same as before but notably different. The scenario we are contemplating here is resumed in the words of the Apostle Paul:

> For I consider that the sufferings of this present time are not worthy to be compared with the glory which shall be revealed in us... For we know that the whole creation groans and labours with birth pangs together until now. And not only they, but we also who have the first fruits of the Spirit, even we ourselves groan within ourselves, eagerly waiting for the adoption, the redemption of our body (Romans 8:18; 22-23).

There are similarities and differences between God's paradise in the Garden of Eden, at the beginning of the Bible, and the New Jerusalem at the end of the Bible. The Garden of Eden was, as the name implies, a garden, with trees and plants. As a result of this abundant green vegetation, our unique atmosphere was created, an atmosphere capable of nurturing and sustaining human life. More than this, it was a garden where God's presence was known and experienced. The New Jerusalem has trees and water, and is also filled with the presence of God.

Though a city, it is unlike earthly cities. It will not be built from the ground up but will descend from heaven. Whereas in the Garden of Eden, God's presence caused the human occupants to feel uncomfortable and ill at ease, through their disobedience, in the New Jerusalem the redeemed will rejoice in God's presence and offer him ceaseless worship. Critically, in contrast to the old earth, which endured the curse and its implications (Genesis 3:17-19), the new earth will be freed from the curse and all its ensuing drudgery and sweat-laden toil (Revelation 22:3).

In the new heaven and earth, the garden is replaced by a city, albeit with several notable botanical features, including life sustaining water and fruit-bearing trees; so, we could call it a *garden city*. A redeemed community set within God's renewed creation. It is towards this same city that the Old Testament pioneers will progress by their faith, together with the saints who have followed them through the pages of history (Hebrews 11:10, 16).

Isaiah, with his God-given ability, saw from distant times what kind of world this would be, a world in which God is known throughout creation: "For the earth shall be full of the knowledge of the Lord, as the waters cover the sea" (Isaiah 11:9).

We believe that all this will happen on planet Earth because to replace the old with something entirely new and other, is not to redeem the old, but to reject it. God has shown us again and again that he takes back the old and perseveres with it, to create something new and beautiful for his pleasure and delight. He does not cast it aside because it is marred or imperfect. The same applies to us human beings. The central message of the gospel is redemption, not rejection.

So far, I have sought to establish by weight of evidence and probability where and what heaven is. Is it somewhere in the vast expanse of the created universe or in some abstract location beyond time and space? If it is to be found in the former, then planet Earth must be a leading contender. If the latter, then that may be harder to equate with the evidence before us.

Heaven can, of course, be an inward state based on the firm assurance of our eternal salvation through Jesus Christ. This is perhaps the most important aspect of heavenly bliss, with questions regarding its whereabouts occupying a place of secondary importance. The reality of heaven is, after all, an eternal dimension outside of time and space or where time, as we know it, ceases to exist.

There is also the related expression, *eternal life* that is found throughout the Gospel of John. In this sense, the writer's meaning is less about timeless life and more about quality of life in God's presence, the gift of God to those who believe in and accept Jesus as Saviour and Lord. This is life which embraces both the qualitative and quantitative dimensions of our existence now and when time transitions to eternity. Towards the end of his ministry, Jesus shares with his disciples the news that troubled times lie ahead when he will be taken from them, but he also opens to them the prospect of a future beyond this period of separation:

> And if I go and prepare a place for you, I will come again and receive you to myself; that where I am, there you may be also (John 14:3).

The sense here is of always being with the Lord. As the Apostle Paul says:

> For if we live, we live to the Lord, and if we die, we die to the Lord. Therefore, whether we live or die, we are the Lord's (Romans 14:8).

Robert Haldane explains what this means, when he says, "Our bodies are the Lord's, and will be preserved by him till the resurrection, when in glory they shall be given back to us; and our souls, in the presence of God, will have happiness and glory till that period shall arrive" (<u>The Epistle to the Romans</u>, p.599).

And, to the dying thief on the cross, Jesus said: "Assuredly, I say to you, today you will be with me in paradise" (Luke 23:43).

Time and eternity

This leads us to another point. How should we equate *this today* with dying and, also, with the resurrection of the dead? Paul gives the impression that the dead will be raised together on the Day of Resurrection and that for now they are in a state comparable to sleep. They are to all intents and purposes already in Paradise. When they awake, it will seem that no time at all had passed since they died. Because they have already transitioned to eternity, where time is no longer perceived.

It would now be helpful to join up the different parts of the jigsaw to give a fuller picture regarding heaven and the afterlife.

In the Bible, there are different contributors to this theme, including Paul. In a pivotal passage, this is what he has to say:

> But I do not want you to be ignorant, brethren, concerning those who have fallen asleep, lest you sorrow as others who have no hope. If we believe that Jesus died and rose again, even so God will bring with him those who sleep in Jesus. For this, we say to you by the word of the Lord, that we who are alive and remain until the coming of the Lord will by no means precede those who are asleep. For the Lord himself will descend from heaven with a shout, with the voice of an archangel, and with the trumpet of God. And the dead in Christ will rise

first. Then we who are alive and remain shall be caught up together with them in the clouds to meet the Lord in the air. And thus, we shall always be with the Lord. Therefore comfort one another with these words (1 Thessalonians 4:13-18).

This passage has to do with the coming of Christ, the rapture, and the resurrection of the dead. For a moment, let us think again about the resurrection of the dead and the *today* of which Jesus spoke from the cross when responding to the penitent thief. What did Jesus mean by '*today*'? It may help to think of the passage of time during our sleep at night. When we wake up during the night and open our eyes in the darkness, we have little idea of what time it is until we check a clock or our watch and are often surprised to find that many hours had passed since we went to sleep. When under a general anaesthetic this lack of awareness of the passage of time is even more acute. Under a general anaesthetic, our consciousness is switched off so that our brain cannot send pain signals to the rest of our body, allowing for surgery to take place. This is a simulation of death without dying. Under general anaesthetic, we cannot breathe unaided and so need to be placed on a respirator. Thankfully, this is also carried out once we are unconscious.

With the aid of these examples, we can draw parallels with our dead state and our relative lack of awareness compared with our conscious state. Paul says that in the twinkling of an eye... we shall be changed (1 Corinthians 15:52).

The sense here is *in a moment of time* or *in an instant*. Falling back on science, Einstein explained that time moves differently for objects in motion compared with objects at rest. It is said that a watched kettle never boils. And when waiting for important news or a train or bus that is running late, time appears to pass more slowly.

As we grow older, time appears to pass more quickly. On the other hand, how often have we heard it said or have said so ourselves: How time flies! Our awareness of time is both apparent and relative, and according to Einstein's Theory of General Relativity, time itself moves at different rates.

The only constant is the speed of light which is the same for every observer anywhere in the world. According to Einstein's theory, time does not pass any more than space does. It is we who pass through time, as we do through space. Of all created life forms, only humans can measure time in intervals of seconds, minutes and hours or think of time in terms of past, present, and future.

The Apostle Peter makes an interesting observation concerning God's concept of time, insofar as for God one day is as a thousand years and a thousand years as one day (2 Peter 3:8). This would make sense and is consistent with our knowledge of God, who exists outside of time yet has entered our world of time and space. In the same manner, his kingdom is now and, also, in the future, where time and eternity merge. From God's perspective, past, present, and future are compressed into a single human moment.

As I have already indicated, before his impending physical departure from Earth, Jesus told his disciples that he would go and prepare a place for them in his Father's house. Here is the essence of what Jesus said:

> I go to prepare a place for you. And if I go and prepare a place for you, I will come again and receive you to myself; where I am, there you may be also (John 14:2b-3).

A Brazilian pastor and theologian, René Kivitz, has argued that here the words of Jesus refer to his death and resurrection, and not to heaven or his second coming, (Quebrando Paradigmas, pp.43-46). I am not convinced that this exegesis flows naturally from the context of Jesus' conversation with his disciples and would tend to go along with those Bible scholars who suggest that these words do have an eschatological nuance.

There is, nonetheless, some difference of opinion among these scholars as to whether the place referred to here by Jesus is temporary or permanent. We have maintained so far in this book that heaven is a temporary resting place for believers who have died and are presently sleeping in the Lord, but it is the *new* heaven that is the ultimate destination of the redeemed. Professor Tasker is of the opinion that Jesus is speaking in the context of "a permanent home where there is room for all believers" (The Gospel According to St. John, p.171).

Furthermore, the idea of multiple dwellings, as per the description given by Jesus, does seem to resonate with the concept of a populated city, rather than an in-transit-resting place for the departed. And I rather think that Jesus would have wanted to focus on this aspect of the future, in that all-important conversation with his close disciples.

A different kind of kingdom

In view of what will follow shortly, I want to state briefly here that, as things stand, heaven and earth are not one and the same thing. The reason for stating what is apparently self-evident will become clear in a moment. Jesus, himself, made a clear distinction between heaven and earth. For example, in the model prayer that he taught his disciples, Jesus says: "Your will be done on Earth as it is in heaven" (Matthew 6:10; Luke 11:2).

Heaven and earth are two different spheres. However, one must not exaggerate their separateness. The two are bound together both in our experience of them and in their respective destinies. Both can be experienced now, and both will be made new. The distinction between heaven and earth is also found in Jesus' response to Pilate, when questioned by him about his kingship. In reply, Jesus answers the Roman procurator: "My kingdom is not of this world" (John 18:36).

Even though God's kingdom and this world are clearly different, they are indeed not entirely separate. I say this because heaven is the realm of God's kingdom and where God's will is done on Earth, there is revealed to us the meaning of heaven and, to some extent, the experience of heaven.

So, what is the nature of this heavenly reality so far as we are concerned? The opening words of the Lord's Prayer are addressed to God in heaven: "In this manner, therefore, pray: Our Father in heaven" (Matthew 6:9).

This does not imply that God is removed from us or somewhere else, or that heaven is in some distant part of the universe. Heaven is where God is. It is his dwelling place, where his presence is most keenly felt. This is what gives heaven its distinctiveness though not separateness from Earth. That is because God is also present in the world. We are reminded that in the moments before his ascension to heaven, Jesus gave this assurance to his disciples: "Lo, I am with you, always" (Matthew 28:20).

And where Jesus is, God is also. Jesus not only represents God to us and us to God he is also *Immanuel*, God with us.

By now, we will have seen that the kingdom of God is not a kingdom that we are meant to understand in a geographical or territorial sense; that is a kingdom with geographic boundaries like those of nation-states, many of which sadly have been drawn artificially by European governments without regard for local and regional tribal or ethnic identities. God's kingdom is a universal kingdom, present in the lives of all who confess Jesus as Saviour and Lord and who do his will, wherever they happen to be on Earth. The kingdom of God is both a present and future reality, indeed, as it has been since the beginning of the gospel of Jesus Christ:

> Now after John was put in prison, Jesus came to Galilee, preaching the gospel of the kingdom of God, and saying, "The time is fulfilled and the kingdom of God is at hand. Repent, and believe in the gospel" (Mark 1:14-15).

The dawn of the kingdom had already arrived but, paradoxically, was still to come, as captured in the Apostle John's glimpse of heaven, when the New Jerusalem descends from heaven and God's perfect rule is enacted on Earth as it is in heaven. This will take place when heaven and earth become one, as a bride and her husband. We are reminded of this in the following:

Then I, John, saw the holy city, New Jerusalem, coming down out of heaven from God, prepared as a bride adorned for her husband (Revelation 21:2).

There was nothing in the words and actions of Jesus during his Galilean ministry, or at any other time, that satisfied the aspirations of those who expected the coming Messiah to bring about a new political reality by way of some kind of military action. His direct response to a question about his claims to kingship put to an end any such thoughts. It was a question intended to entrap Jesus, but his reply was, as always, well considered, and full of wisdom. Asking for a Roman coin he asked whose image was engraved on it. When his inquisitors replied *Caesar*, Jesus gave the answer: "Render to Caesar the things that are Caesar's, and to God the things that are God's" (Mark 12:17; Matthew 22:15-22).

However, the expectation of the Jewish militants was that Jesus would be instrumental in achieving the overthrow of Roman rule, but such an expectation was frustrated and disappointed. Their attempt to achieve this in the Jewish revolt of 66-70 AD brought only disaster upon the nation and a further attempt of the same in AD 132, served only to bring about the complete end of the Jewish nation, together with its cherished institutions. This loss of Jewish nationhood, together with their land, lasted for almost another 2000 years.

As we have seen, God's kingdom is both present and future. It is here and now, but to be fully revealed in the future. What does this mean? As things stand, God's kingdom is already being established on Earth. It was with this in mind that Jesus taught us to pray saying, "Your kingdom come, your will be done on Earth *as it is in heaven"* (italics mine).

There is a parallelism here, which is also found in the psalms and other poetic literature in the Bible. Wherever God's will is being done, there, also, is the reality of God's kingdom. They are one and the same thing. There is, likewise, a direct relationship between God's kingdom and heaven. To do God's will is to give expression to and advance the kingdom of God on Earth, and to establish a connection between heaven and earth.

Heaven touches earth

Jesus taught us how to pray and in so doing, showed us clearly the relationship between heaven and earth. This same Jesus is now at the right hand of God the Father, ascended and glorified. Jesus was with the Father in heaven from eternity, until he took on human form and was born in Bethlehem of Judea.

In his high priestly prayer (John 17), Jesus longed to be restored to his former glory in heaven. We cannot escape the fact Jesus was aware of the existence of heaven and he was familiar with this unseen reality. To return to that place from which he had come, Jesus had to fulfil his mission on Earth. And as Jesus well knew, the way back to heaven was the Via Dolorosa, the way of the Cross. This is true of all who long to be with him in heaven.

For this reason, the Apostle Paul desired above all else to share in the sufferings of Jesus and to know the power of his resurrection (Philippians 3:10). To share in the sufferings of Jesus is what it means to take up one's cross daily and follow him. These sufferings are those we experience as a direct result of following Jesus, because to follow him invariably means to go against the tide of this world.

After his resurrection, Jesus appeared to his disciples for forty days. His physical appearance had changed. His presence was no longer limited to time and space. He came and went without warning. This naturally left the disciples confused and frustrated. On one occasion, they decided to return to their previous occupation and go fishing (John 21). To my mind, by this time, Jesus had already ascended to heaven. He had already returned to the Father. This is certainly the impression given by the Apostle John in his recording of the resurrection appearances. If this is so, and if we follow this line of thought, then Jesus was in heaven on the occasions when he met with his disciples after the resurrection.

It is neither logical nor reasonable to think that Jesus was coming and going between heaven and earth during those forty days. What is generally thought to be his ascension was, in fact, his last visible appearance to his disciples on Earth. Once ascended, Jesus remained ascended. This was and is definitive until his return in glory, at the consummation of all things. When Jesus met with his disciples, for brief moments, he was bringing heaven to earth, as was the case at that unforgettable breakfast on the beach prepared for the disciples by Jesus himself (John 21:9-14).

We can therefore say, with confidence, that where Jesus is there also is heaven. To be in the presence of Jesus, is to be in heaven itself. Of course, this has interesting implications and begs the question as to heaven's actual location in time and space.

One of my favourite Old Testament passages is Jacob's dream at Bethel in which he sees a ladder stretching from earth to heaven, with God's angels ascending and descending on it. In his dream, heaven and earth are touching by way of the ladder and God's ascending and descending heavenly angels. This is, of course, a two-dimensional view of what Jacob saw in his dream. We could also say, without equivocation that the angels were, in fact, *coming and going* between the two realms. Here is the story as recorded in the Book of Genesis:

> Now Jacob left Beersheba and went towards Haran. So he came to a certain place and stayed there all night, because the sun had set. And he took one of the stones of that place and put it at his head, and he lay down in that place to sleep. Then he dreamed, and behold, a ladder was set up on the earth, and its top reached to heaven; and there the angels of God were ascending and descending on it... Then Jacob awoke from his sleep and said, "Surely the Lord is in this place, and I did not know it." And he was afraid and said, "How awesome is this place! This is none other than the house of God, and this is the gate of heaven!" (28:10-12; 16-17).

In no way are we trying to redefine heaven but rather, we are seeking to know exactly what the Bible teaches us about heaven. An interesting point has been made by N. T. Wright, when he says that heaven is but the "thin curtain between God's space and ours" (Surprised by Hope, p.66). If this is so, heaven is not as far away as we might imagine. It is not so much *up in the sky* as *across the way*. This may come as a surprise to some, but it is possibly a more accurate way of describing where heaven is in relation to us.

Here is another description of where heaven is, from a sermon delivered at St. Paul's Cathedral after the death of King Edward VII. This sermon has now become famous as a poem, often read at funerals. The opening two stanzas read as follows:

Death is nothing at all.
It does not count.
I have only slipped away into the next room.
Nothing has happened.
Everything remains exactly as it was.
I am I, and you are you,
and the old life that we lived so fondly together is untouched, unchanged.
Whatever we were to each other that we are still.
Henry Scott-Holland (1847-1918).

Though in, some respects, this is not to be taken too literally, the writer suggests that heaven is nearer than we imagine. The thought that a long journey is involved in our transit from this life to the next is absent here. The sense is of continuity and hopefulness. I have for a long time felt that these words were wishful thinking - an attempt to comfort the bereaved but without biblical basis.

More recently, I have come to think differently about this poem, because, at heart, it is not so far from my own thinking about dying and death. There seems to me to be no biblical reason to impose a huge distance between the here and now and the next world. Maybe recent exploration of the universe has tipped things in this direction. And not only this. Scripture, itself, does not seem to suggest the idea of remoteness or otherworldliness to the extent that many of us may have presupposed.

Tom Wright is helpful again at this point when he says, "Heaven and earth are not distinct spheres separated by a great geographical or ontological distance, but actually overlap and interlock" (New Heavens, New Earth, p.16). In the same volume, Bishop Wright supports the notion that heaven is, for the departed, a resting place until Christ returns. This, he reminds us, is grounded in the Jewish understanding of Paradise as "the temporary place of rest before the rising again from the dead" (Ibid. p.22). We are reminded once again of the words Jesus spoke to the penitent thief on the cross: "Today you will be with me in paradise" (Luke 23:43).

These words are beautifully reassuring, because they explain to us, in a simple poignant statement, that Jesus is with us in death as much as life and that death is nothing other than a resting place, as we await the day of resurrection.

According to Paul, those who have died in the Lord are in the presence of the Lord until he returns: "We are confident, yes, well pleased rather to be absent from the body and to be present with the Lord" (2 Corinthians 5:8).

But what happens after we arrive in heaven? Paul provides us with an answer to this question. He points to the resurrection of the dead and the nature of the resurrection body, which will be continuous with our earthly body, insofar as we will be able to recognise one another, even though our bodies will be substantially different: "So also is the resurrection of the dead. The body is sown... a natural body, it is raised a spiritual body" (1 Corinthians 15:42, 44).

To visualise what this might mean, we need only to recall the change in Jesus' body after his resurrection. It was different without doubt, but, even so, the disciples slowly recognised him through the mists of their incredulity.

And what of those who are still alive when Jesus returns? Once more, we can turn to God's word for the answer. As it says, they will be transformed without experiencing death:

> Behold, I tell you a mystery: We shall not all sleep, but we shall all be changed – in a moment, in the twinkling of an eye, at the last trumpet. For the trumpet will sound, and the dead will be raised incorruptible, and we shall be changed (1 Corinthians 15:51-52).

This resonates with what Paul also said previously when he wrote to the church in Thessalonica:

> Then we who are alive and remain shall be caught up together with them in the clouds to meet the Lord in the air. And thus, we shall always be with the Lord (1 Thessalonians 4:17).

This leads us to the Millennium and, also, to several important questions: Is the thousand-year rule of Christ on Earth a symbolic amount of time? If so, is it indeterminate? The Book of Revelation is laden with language that may seem strange to us and is open to various interpretations. If it is to be read in a literal sense, what then happens at the end of this time of rule? The Bible tells us that Satan will be let loose for a short period and then finally thrown into the lake of fire where he will remain forever (Revelation 20:10). This would represent the final overthrow of the powers of darkness and evil. Beyond this, we are not given any further information regarding the saints but may conclude that the joy of salvation continues uninterrupted. For it is then that the New Jerusalem will descend from heaven and those who had professed Christ as Saviour and Lord will be invited to enter the city:

> Blessed are those who do his commandments, that they may have the right to the tree of life, and may enter through the gates into the city (Revelation 22:14).

Now, indeed, we stand at the gates of eternity, and can hear the final invitation to the saints before they enter: "And let him who thirsts come. And whoever desires, let him take the water of life freely" (Revelation 22:17).

And, so, the saints enter the holy city, the New Jerusalem, whose gates are open day and night, and where they will reign with him forever and ever (Revelation 21:25; 22:5).

Paul, when writing to the church in Philippi, regards those who belong to Christ as already having received the status of citizens of heaven:

> For our citizenship is in heaven, from which we also eagerly wait for the Saviour, the Lord Jesus Christ, who will transform our lowly body that it may be conformed to his glorious body, according to the working by which he is able even to subdue all things to himself (Philippians 3:20-21).

As citizens of heaven, we are by extension citizens of the holy city, the New Jerusalem, the city of heaven come down to Earth. As it were, we are counted as having a passport to heaven, issued under the authority of King Jesus, the Lamb who sits on the throne of God (Revelation 3:21).

It is worth noting, in parenthesis, that the Holy City is described by John in some considerable detail. The general description and measurements given are symbolic of perfection, as one might rightly imagine heaven to be (Revelation 21:9-27). So, what will heaven be like? In Revelation Chapter 21, we get a glimpse of how it really is. Firstly, we come to the measurements. These are to perfection.

An exact cube whose dimensions are multiples of twelve, representing the twelve tribes of Israel, supported by the foundation of the twelve apostles. The impressive thickness of the city walls guarantees absolute security to all who reside within those walls. The measurements are here given by human standards but, whether they are to be taken literally or symbolically, the clear implication is that there is room within those walls for all who have given their allegiance to Jesus. My personal impression is that the numbers are symbolic, though descriptive of the new reality which awaits us.

In the city, there will be no sorrow, suffering or death. There will be no temple, or night or sea. For God's presence will fill the city, and he will give light to the city. Moreover, the city will be free of malice and evil, where the people of God will enjoy the immediacy of the presence of God forever. It will be the antithesis of the world, as we know it today. We catch a glimpse of this new and quite different reality in John's vision:

> After these things, I looked and behold, a great multitude which no one could number, of all nations, tribes, peoples, and tongues, standing before the

throne and before the Lamb... (Then one of the elders said to me), "they are before the throne of God, and serve him day and night in his temple. And he who sits on the throne will dwell among them. They shall neither hunger any more nor thirst any more; the sun shall not strike them, nor any heat; for the Lamb who is in the midst of the throne will shepherd them and lead them to living fountains of waters. And God will wipe away every tear from their eyes" (Revelation 7:9, 15-17).

There are several themes here that are repeated later in Chapters 21 and 22. They are the Lamb, the throne, living water, the absence of grief and want, and the service and worship of the people of God. These themes are indicative of the future that God is preparing for us, and which the church awaits with eager anticipation. But the church is not simply waiting for this to happen; it also declares that this will happen and does so whenever it meets around the Lord's Table.

Wade Eaton, in his contribution to a collection of essays entitled <u>The Trial of Faith</u> addresses this situation in the following way:

"It is generally recognised that the Eucharist is closely related to the significance and purpose of Jesus' death; it dramatises, as it were, how that death was for us. What is less commonly grasped is that this insight is only a part of the understanding of the primitive Church. The Eucharistic liturgy is not only oriented towards a saving event in the past; it is also oriented towards the future, that time when God intends to transform the whole human world in the image of his Son." Paul expresses this double focus most concisely: "For as often as you eat this bread and drink this cup, you proclaim the Lord's death till he comes" (1 Corinthians 11:26).

For the church, as it takes part in this central act of worship, there is a looking back to the cross: "Do this in remembrance of me." But there is also a sense of looking forward in anticipation to future cosmic events: these are the return of Jesus and the coming out of heaven of the New Jerusalem, adorned as a bride for her husband. This is the perfected church, the successor to Israel, the abode of the risen Lord. God will indeed make his dwelling among us, and we will be with him forever (Revelation 21:2-3).

I think it is justified, at this point, to bring into play what David Bosch has to say about the church, in the wider context of proclamation and mission. He asserts that the present and future aspects of God's rule motivate us to give the necessary distance to this world whilst being involved in its transformation. By declaring the gospel of present salvation and future hope, we identify with the birth pains of God's new creation (Transforming Mission, p.510).

Seven centuries before John's heavenly vision, the prophet Ezekiel had a vision of a new temple (chapters 40-44). In this vision, he is given details concerning the temple's rules of practice and the precise measurements of its physical structure, although this probably references the restoration of the Jerusalem temple following the Babylonian exile. It is significant that in John's vision of the New Jerusalem, there is, in fact, no physical temple: "But I saw no temple in it, for the Lord God Almighty and the Lamb are its temple" (Revelation 21:22).

A temple is understood to be the location of God's presence. King Solomon, when he dedicated the temple in Jerusalem, was acutely aware that God was greater than even the greatest building built with human hands. This he laid bare in his dedicatory prayer:

> But will God indeed dwell on the earth? Behold, heaven and the heaven of heavens cannot contain you.

How much less this temple which I have built! (1 Kings 8:27).

God is omnipresent; his presence is ubiquitous and knows no bounds in heaven or earth. For this reason, there is no need for a temple in the celestial city; the entire city is a holy place populated by God's people, where the sense of his all-pervading presence is known and enjoyed beyond measure.

For the very reason that there is no temple in the heavenly Jerusalem, so neither will there be any altar or religious ritual, choreographed by worship leaders and priests directing our attention toward God. The trappings of earthly worship will no longer be necessary because there, God is everywhere and by everyone adored in spontaneous and everlasting worship.

For further personal reflection or group discussion:

How would you compare the experience of humans in the Garden of Eden with their future in the heavenly city?

In what ways is it possible to experience heaven on Earth?

Where can we see signs of God's kingdom around us?

What did Jesus mean when he said to the thief on the cross, "Today you will be with me in Paradise"?

Why will there be no temple in the New Jerusalem?

CHAPTER FIVE
NOT SO OTHER WORLDLY

Although in the Bible, the earth is indicated as the location of the New Jerusalem, it will be a different earth from the present one. The earth will be refashioned and changed from how we know it now. The present earth is a place marred by sin and our human negative impact on it, a sign of our rebellion against God. This earth, abused and neglected by those who were called to be good stewards of it, will be transformed by God and that beyond recognition (cf. Jeremiah 18:1-4).

The new earth will once again be pleasing to God, as it was in the beginning: "Then God saw everything that he had made, and indeed it was very good" (Genesis 1:31).

That cannot be said now as the destructive and disfiguring processes, initiated and prompted by the actions of the first humans in the first garden, and from which they were ultimately banished, see no sign of abating. But when will God's redemptive work begin? It has already begun. And this with the birth of Jesus, his baptism in the river Jordan, his Galilean ministry and death on the cross; and by his resurrection, ascension, and exaltation to the right hand of God. Therefore, God has given undisputable signs to this effect, and the confirmation that his purposes are unstoppable. However, the timing of some significant future events, including the cosmic event of the return of Christ (to which we shall come in a moment), remain the exclusive preserve of God the Father (Mark 13:32).

Doubts and questions

After his resurrection on the first Easter Sunday, Jesus met with his disciples and again on several other occasions during the following forty days, including one last time before his ascension when the conversation went as follows:

> Therefore, when they had come together, they asked him, saying, "Lord, will you at this time restore the kingdom to Israel?" And he said to them, "It is not for you to know times or seasons which the Father has put in his own authority. But you shall receive power when the Holy Spirit has come upon you; and you shall be witnesses to me in Jerusalem, and in all Judea and Samaria, and to the end of the earth" (Acts 1:6-8).

Evidently, the disciples still had some doubts and questions about the nature and purpose of Jesus' mission. What kind of kingdom was to be installed, and when? Though Jesus would not be drawn on the subject and no further clarification is given, he explained that they would receive power from on high to continue his mission on Earth, beginning in Jerusalem. The nature of the kingdom which the disciples had in mind was still different from that which Jesus contemplated. As, also, was the promised power by which their mission would be accomplished. Instead of destructive power sufficient to overthrow the Roman occupation of Palestine, the disciples were given the power to heal, restore and forgive.

Together with the message they preached, the signs that followed brought hope and assurance to empty and broken lives. Although history has a way of repeating itself, as empires rise and fall and dictators come and go, it is at the same time on a linear trajectory, moving towards a final and glorious outcome. And, in this respect, there are plentiful signs in our own generation that the end game is about to be played out. Below is a sample to give us the flavour of the progression of events associated with the close of this present age:

> When you hear of wars and rumours of wars, do not be troubled; for such things must happen, but the end is not yet. For nation will rise against nation, and kingdom against kingdom. And there will be earthquakes in various places, and there will be famines and troubles. These are the beginnings of sorrows. And the gospel must first be preached to all the nations... In those days there will be tribulation, such as has not been from the beginning of the creation which God created until this time, nor ever shall be. But in those days, after the tribulation, the sun will be darkened, and the moon will not give its light. Then they will see the Son of Man coming in the clouds with great power and glory. And then he will send his angels, and gather his elect from the four winds, from the farthest part of earth to the farthest part of heaven (Mark 13:7-8, 10, 19, 24, 26-27).

This passage has elements in common with Jewish apocalyptic circulating at the time, which Mark may have included here. But the reference to the Son of Man gives reason to believe that this part of the discourse came from the lips of Jesus, himself. In support of this view is the fact of a similar saying of Jesus, at a different time and place, in response to Nathanael, recorded in the Gospel of John (1:51).

A key issue here, however, is the time and place of the tribulation. It would appear to precede the coming of the Son of Man and the gathering in of the elect 'from the farthest part of earth to the farthest part of heaven' (Mark 13:27). Those who are presently at rest in heaven and those who will remain until the time of the Lord's return. The tribulation appears to be directed at God's elect but also the whole earth is affected by it. At the same time, for the sake of the elect, the days of the tribulation will be shortened (Mark 13:20).

The well-known adage has it that 'things will get worse before they get better' and perhaps gives an answer to those who are troubled and confused by the situation in the world today. Why is there so much suffering and why are there so many wars and conflicts? These questions can be answered in two ways: firstly, we live in a fallen world which is prone to these things. They are the consequence of human decisions and choices from the beginning of time. Suffering is sometimes undoubtedly self-inflicted, but not always. Natural disasters are often down to the fact that creation is involved in this *fallenness* through no fault of its own (excuse the play on words in connection with the natural occurrence of earthquakes).

Secondly, these things can be considered as destined to happen, as foreseen in John's unforgettable vision of heaven. Here he sees a multitude which no one could number, from all nations, tribes, peoples, and tongues, dressed in white robes, standing before the throne of God. These are the ones who had come out of the great tribulation, washed their robes and made them white in the blood of the Lamb (Revelation 7:9-14).

Though it would seem, come what may, tribulations of many different kinds await us, so does the prize for which we can strive. This is the incomparable reward of patient, trusting, and sacrificial living before God, throughout our varied earthly journeys in the direction of the Promised Land. The years of wandering in the desert wilderness could have been greatly curtailed had God's people believed the report of Joshua and Caleb and not heeded the advice of their companions on the reconnaissance trip to access the situation ahead. Jesus had much to say about the future of the world and our own futures. We cannot separate these futures and, inevitably, they will pan out together, as the closing stages of history continue to unfold.

The demise of the sun is also predicted, not only by first-century theologians like John but also by twenty-first century scientists. It might come as a relief to know that this celestial event will not happen for another six billion years. When it does happen and whatever may ensue, another event, the appearance of the celestial city coming out of heaven, will eclipse even the splendour of the Sun (Revelation 21:23).

As I have maintained throughout our reflections, the different eschatological passages in Scripture are there to be reconciled, though not in a forced or artificial way. What I am saying is they should be read alongside one another to be rightly interpreted and understood. An example of this would be the *Son of Man* in Mark 13 and the eschatological figure *like the Son of Man* in Daniel Chapter 7. Did Jesus have in mind the supernatural figure described in Daniel when referring to his own return? Are these two connected in any way? It is certainly tempting to make a connection here and with some justification. Edward J. Young would seem to agree when he asserts that, "it was this vision that our Lord had in mind when He referred to Himself as the Son of man" (The New Bible Commentary Revised, p.697).

The manner of his appearing *in the clouds* is identical in both instances. Jesus had adopted the custom of referring to himself as the Son of Man throughout his ministry, a title used by him alone and no other, except Stephen (Acts 7:55-56). In his vision within the veil of heaven, Stephen explicitly identifies the Son of Man with Jesus which proved to be the final straw leading to his stoning by the religious mob.

The followers of Jesus customarily used the traditional title of Rabbi (Teacher) so only Jesus would have understood the connection of the title Son of Man with the eternal God, the *Ancient of Days*, from whom he received "dominion and glory and a kingdom, that all peoples, nations, and languages should serve him" (Daniel 7:14a). The text from Daniel fits well with another description of this future cosmic event:

> Behold, he is coming with clouds, and every eye will see him, and they also who pierced him. And all the tribes of the earth will mourn because of him. Even so, Amen. "I am the Alpha and the Omega, the Beginning and the End," says the Lord, "who is and who was and who is to come, the Almighty" (Revelation 1:7-8).

There is a significant chain of corroborating evidence from Scripture and, moreover, from Jesus himself, to link the events described in Daniel 7 to the Parousia; that is the return of Jesus in the clouds with the holy angels, in great power and glory, when the trumpet shall sound, and the dead will rise (1 Corinthians 15:52). What a wonderful spectacle that will be and one which we can anticipate with eagerness and confidence (1 Corinthians 1:7).

And, so, we arrive at another topic. As we have already seen, in the Fourth Gospel, the Apostle John characteristically alludes to the concept of *eternal* life (Gk. aionios zoe). Although this term is often translated from the original Greek as *everlasting* life, it should not be restricted to or understood as merely future life, and certainly not life without end, divorced from fullness of life (John 10:10). Jesus, himself, defines eternal life in these terms:

> And this is eternal life, that they may know you, the only true God, and Jesus Christ whom you have sent (John 17:3).

Eternal life is not a natural human attribute but is God's gift to those who are joined to him in a relationship made possible by Jesus Christ. This life translates into a purposeful and abundant life to all those who put their trust in him and the power of his saving work on the cross.

Most interpreters of John's Gospel regard eternal life in this way, as lived in the present, but also life which continues as a future reality for all of time and beyond time. The emphasis, however, is always on the quality of life rather than its duration. The sense is that one can enjoy eternal life here and now; that is, the immediate reality of heaven on Earth.

The Apostle John now alludes to the relationship between heaven and earth, as he records, in his Gospel, the first words of Jesus to Nathanael, also known as Bartholomew, one of the twelve disciples.

> The following day Jesus wanted to go to Galilee, and he found Philip and said to him, "Follow me." Now Philip was from Bethsaida, the city of Andrew and Peter. Philip found Nathanael and said to him, "We have found him of whom Moses in the law, and also the prophets, wrote – Jesus of Nazareth, the son of Joseph." And Nathanael said to him, "Can any good come out of Nazareth?" Philip said to him, "Come and see." Jesus saw Nathanael coming towards him, and said to him, "Behold an Israelite indeed, in whom is no guile!" Nathanael said to him, "How do you know me?" Jesus answered and said to him, "Before Philip called you, when you were under the fig tree, I saw

you." Nathanael answered and said to him, "Rabbi, you are the Son of God. You are the King of Israel!" Jesus answered and said to him, "Because I said to you, 'I saw you under the fig tree,' do you believe? You will see greater things than these." And he said to him, "Most assuredly, I say to you, hereafter you shall see heaven open, and the angels of God ascending and descending upon the Son of Man" (John 1:43-51).

An analysis of the Gospels concerning the Son of Man sayings will reveal that Jesus appropriated the title Son of Man to himself in connection with his earthly ministry (Mark 10:45), the cross and resurrection (Mark 8:31; 10:32-34), and his coming again (Mark 13:24-27).

Some critics claim that when Jesus is referring to the end times, he is pointing to another and not to himself. This is a false dichotomy and does not represent a natural interpretation of the text, which strongly suggests the identification between Jesus and the Son of Man. Where the identification is obvious, in texts connected to his ministry and Passion, these words are attributed to early Christian writers conferring on Jesus this title. In other words, the church is held to have superimposed on Jesus a false identification with the supernatural figure of the Son of Man.

Among others, Joseph Ratzinger believes that it was Jesus' intention to identify himself with the Son of Man. And whilst not a product or projection of the faith of the first-century Christian community, the concept was adopted and elaborated by that community. Furthermore, Ratzinger concludes that there is no other explanation for the emergence or survival of the church except for something quite extraordinary, beyond a discussion of titles and who attributed them and to whom they were attributed. That something is the Resurrection, the only explanation for the hope and resilience of the church as it awaits the return of Jesus, the Son of Man. Of course, Ratzinger is by no means alone in making the connection between the resurrection and the emergence and survival of the Christian church. This is the commonly held conviction of all those for whom the resurrection has led to the transformation of their everyday lives.

Often the stories in the Bible are reckoned to be stories and nothing more, as if they had no practical meaning and purpose in the real world. The story of Jacob's ladder may be one such story, beautiful and enthralling as it is, but lacking any attachment to our earthly reality. In fact, nothing could be further from the truth. Jesus did not view the Old Testament stories in this fanciful way. Though the story of Jacob's ladder is based on a dream, it has a clear message for us regarding heaven and where it is in relation to Earth. Perhaps not an everyday experience; the reality does not change. Heaven is closer to us than we are by and large aware.

How to cross over

The words of Jesus to Nathanael explain how heaven and earth will come together. The imagery employed by Jesus is reminiscent of the story of Jacob's ladder in which angels ascended and descended between heaven and earth, to which we have referred. The fact that Jesus made use of this Old Testament story not only authenticates Jacob's dream, but it also explains how heaven on Earth translates into reality.

Commenting on the Nathanael passage, Gordon Campbell gives a pinpoint summary of how this has already come about, when he writes, "Jesus makes the vision real for his new follower, for the link between heaven and earth is none other than Jesus himself" (Breaking Through and Reaching Out. Book 2: A Call to Ignite – Living in the Spirit, p.174).

In support of this connection between heaven and earth is Jesus' declaration that "no one comes to the Father except through me" (John 14:6). Within this context, we learn that Jesus is the true and living way. It is through him that we have access to heaven and its rewards. By the same token, without him, there is no pathway to heaven, and heaven remains as inaccessible as the furthest reaches of the universe.

In the Bible, the word *heavens* in the plural form, usually means the skies above or around us, for example, Genesis 1:1; Psalm 19:1. Heaven in the singular tends to refer to God's abode as in Matthew 6:9. Here, in the Lord's Prayer, Jesus is clearly referring to God's abode, though as we have seen already, this is more than a place in the heavens above; it is more like the totality of the space around us and above us, a reality unseen.

There is much in Scripture that lends to the idea that heaven can be experienced on Earth as an immediate reality, though in its fullest expression, only when all things are subject to Christ as Lord, as envisaged in Paul's letter to the church in the ancient Roman colony of Philippi:

> At the name of Jesus every knee should bow, of those in heaven, and of those on Earth, and of those under the earth; and that every tongue should confess that Jesus Christ is Lord, to the glory of God the Father (Philippians 2:10-11).

Heaven is both an inward and outward experience of the presence of God in our lives. The following adaptation of a Benedictine prayer seems to me to express this reality and is appropriate at this point in our reflection:

Lord of all that is silent and all that is spoken, because our lives are full of detail and deadlines, much to be done and little time in which to do it all, we find few moments in which to enjoy the beauty of the world. To contemplate the fierce endurance of everything that lives, to enter that timeless realm of divine mystery which surrounds us, entered only in silence. Yet we know that this place exists and is close to us. O God, grant us a glimpse of this inner sanctuary, and the desire and calm to dwell there in prayer. As we continue our journey, help us to make more time for study, and more time for silence, that we may hear your voice in our lives. Open us to hear the words of Jesus in new ways, as they were new to those who first heard them.

What we see around us in the natural world inspires wonder and exhilaration, but also the expectation that this, once perfected at his coming will be, simply and unequivocally, heaven on Earth. Leon Morris explains it simply and is to the point: "After the New Jerusalem descends there appears to be no difference between heaven and earth" (The Revelation of St. John: An Introduction and Commentary, p.244). Each infuses the other, in a state of perfect union, above all, characterised by the fullness of the presence of God.

If we bring together the results of scientific exploration and theological insights rooted in Scripture, we find that both are on the same page or, at the very least, saying something very similar. Faith requires intuition, but so does science. Faith is based on a process of experience tested by Scripture; science is based on observation and verification. The way we interpret Scripture has been increasingly influenced by scientific observations. It would be unhelpful, if not unwise, to make statements about the heavens and earth that contradict science, as did the Roman Catholic Church in the Middle Ages when it disagreed with Copernicus, the Polish astronomer, who claimed that the earth revolved around the Sun. For this, he was excommunicated for no less a matter than disagreeing with the church in a matter where science should surely prevail.

Most Christians today accept scientific theories, once proven, and gladly affirm that science is of God, from God and belongs to God. William Paley's Natural Theology was aimed not at refuting science but accommodating science in ways that allowed for both science and theology to be reconciled. Through science, God reveals himself to us in the wonder and mystery of the created world, and through Scripture, his relationship to us and our relationship to the world. On the one hand, science deals with the evidence of objective facts, as far as we understand them at the present time. On the other, faith is *the substance of things hoped for, the evidence of things not seen* (Hebrews 11:1). Both are based on evidence, but different kinds of evidence.

Science is constantly extending the boundaries of knowledge, whereas faith also increases to the extent that God reveals himself to us through contemporary testimony, the testimony of Scripture, and supremely in Jesus Christ. I have found Joseph Ratzinger's book, Jesus of Nazareth, to be surprising in many ways and always thought provoking, much of which is after my own heart. In the section dealing with the Beatitudes, he suggests that a personal seeking after God and the pursuit of justice are the precursors to an encounter with God (p.94). To this, I would add that when we meet with God, in the light of his presence, we find the clarity we need to understand more fully his purposes for us and the planet that has been entrusted to us.

So, we come again to the question which concerns itself with the location of heaven. Where is it? How do we get there? My friend and colleague, Gordon Campbell, brings this whole matter down to earth when he says, "any declaration in God's name has the effect of bringing heaven to earth" (Breaking Through and Reaching Out: Living in the Spirit, p.220).

Thinking of heaven as a reality, involving planet Earth - not only as we know it now but, also, as we are yet to know it - dispenses with totally other worldly conceptions. As mentioned earlier in this book, my understanding of Scripture is generally based on the most natural interpretation of the text. Regarding our future heavenly body, this will not be the body we now have simply resurrected from the grave, but nonetheless it will be a body. We will not be disembodied spirits in the heavenly city; the Apostle Paul makes this quite clear in his first letter to the church in Corinth (15:44). Our natural body will be replaced by a spiritual body, but a body, nonetheless; one that is related to the spirit and serves the needs of the spirit (see Leon Morris, The First Epistle of Paul to the Corinthians, p.228).

In the same manner, concerning our present and future bodily state, Norman Hillyer makes the following observation: "Physical and spiritual indicate the spheres or forms of existence for which the bodies respectively are fitted" (1 and 2 Corinthians, p.1072). There appears to be agreement among scholars to the effect that in heaven our spirit will be embodied. From the perspective of Scripture, we will continue to have shape and form, as well as other personal characteristics, to enable the recognition by others that we are one and the same person as before.

The earth we now inhabit has a significant role in God's future for us. We will be raised bodily for life in this new heavenly, as well as new earthly world. And, bearing in mind the role of the present earth in God's plans for tomorrow, we ought to take special care to exercise responsible dominion over it, using the best of our God-given creative reason and imagination.

Where to from here?

This brings us to another crucial milestone on our journey. Where would we go from here, if life on this planet were to be faced with extinction? There is nowhere else for us to go in our solar system; and to go anywhere else further afield is neither likely nor feasible, except in science fiction. If we do not become disembodied spirits when we die, we will need a new physical place in which to continue our existence. Science can explore human possibilities, but it also defines human limitations. Science and theology are best served as they speak to each other, in pursuit of a dialogue which leads to a fuller understanding of the mystery of the universe and of God, to the extent that he reveals himself to us.

When Jesus returned to heaven, he took with him the physical body with which he was clothed at his birth. Even so, his resurrection body was strangely different. After his resurrection, he was able to pass through closed doors and move from one place to another without any apparent interval of time. His body was recognisable and palpable, though still somehow different. Jesus declared to his astonished disciples, on meeting with them, that his was a real body, not a disembodied spirit (Luke 24.36-43). We can safely conclude that Jesus took with him to heaven a real human body, one which bears the marks of his suffering and crucifixion. I elaborate further on this point in my book, <u>Jesus: Dead or Alive? The evidence</u>, also available from Kingdom Publishers.

The sense of this statement is perfectly captured in the following verse from the hymn, At the Name of Jesus, by Caroline Noel:

Bore it up triumphant
With its human light,
Through all ranks of creatures,
To the central height;
To the throne of Godhead,
To the Father's breast,
Filled it with the glory
Of that perfect rest.

I wish to state as clearly as possible that the physical and spiritual, though separated when we die, will be perfectly united in the new heaven and earth. Of course, the old body is done with, but a new body awaits us. Noel's hymn is based on an early Christian creed, used by the Apostle Paul in Philippians 2:5-11. It expresses well the glorious reality which is guaranteed to us because of the redemptive work of Jesus on the cross, his resurrection and ascension, all of which were underscored by the Godhead, visibly and audibly present, at his baptism in the river Jordan (Matthew 3:13-17).

What he did and what he accomplished on our behalf was to bring to us the awareness and assurance that life on Earth is not the *be all and end all* of human existence. Death is not final. If this were the case, we might be forgiven for thinking we had been short-changed after all our labours and strivings, and after all we had acquired and achieved in this world. It is true that none of our wealth and material achievements can be taken with us when we die. We will have to let it all go. But far better than material possessions, Jesus took with him to heaven our humanity with which he was also clothed at his birth in Bethlehem. However, we need to remember that after he rose from a garden tomb outside Jerusalem, Jesus was clothed in a different kind of flesh and blood which is precisely the resurrection body we shall acquire for citizenship of the New Jerusalem. This is also the nature of the body with which Jesus ascended to heaven at the end of the forty days of his visible appearances to his disciples.

You may recall that the post-ascension appearances of Jesus to the first Christian martyr (Stephen), to Saul of Tarsus (later Paul), and the Apostle John (on the Greek island of Patmos) were clearly of a different order of glory to those appearances between his resurrection and ascension. These were manifestations of his earthly self now united to his pre-incarnate self: "I am he who lives, and was dead, and behold, I am alive for evermore" (Revelation 1:18a).

We, who follow Jesus now, will not lose our essential self or our unique identity in the heavenly Jerusalem. All that we are now, we will be, but risen to a new level of self and being. There, in that perfected state, we will be able to offer perfect praise to him who is worthy of all worship.

While death is a valley to be travelled through and a river to be crossed, the future beyond that river is bright and glorious. And it will be so because Jesus walked this same valley and crossed this river and has gone before us. Because he did just that and because he lives, we can believe in tomorrow! In the words of the Apostle Paul:

> O Death, where is your sting? O Death, where is your victory? Thanks be to God, who gives us the victory through our Lord Jesus Christ (1 Corinthians 15:55, 57).

The Bible is clear that when we die, we will not migrate to some distant place in the cosmos but, rather, we shall be called into the near presence of God. Then on the day of resurrection, we shall be clothed in our new body, one fit for heaven on Earth.

For further personal reflection or group discussion:

What do you think are the signs of the end times?

Jesus promised that tribulation would come to the world. Can troubled times bring assurance that this promise is being fulfilled?

Why do you think Jesus chose for himself the title, Son of Man? Why did this lead to his death on the cross and to the stoning of Stephen, the first Christian martyr? (see Acts 7:56).

Is eternal life something for the world to come only? How did Jesus define eternal life?

Can you see any similarities between the creation story in Genesis and modern scientific theory, as to how the earth began?

CHAPTER SIX
ARE WE ALONE IN THE UNIVERSE?

Having earlier contemplated the universe and planet Earth's place within the incomprehensible vastness of space, the burning question is, Are we alone? There are up to 400 billion stars in our galaxy, the Milky Way, and over 100 billion galaxies in the known universe, many larger than our own. The Andromeda Galaxy, the one nearest to the Milky Way, is over twice the size at 220,000 light years across. The total number of stars in the observable universe has been calculated at 10 billion trillion (Leonor Sierra, University of Rochester). Now, that's a lot of stars!

For us to have some idea of what this means, it has been estimated that there are more stars in the universe than there are grains of sand on all of Earth's beaches (Simon Driver, ABC Science). The nearest star to our sun is 4.24 light years away or 25 trillion miles (Erik Gregersen, Encyclopaedia Britannica). As we can see, despite their great number, stars are not exactly packed tightly together in the sky. These numbers will give us something by which to measure the enormity of the universe, though, at the same time, they serve only to confound us even more.

To give us a notion of the potential for intelligent life existing beyond the earth, there are more than five thousand identified exoplanets (planets orbiting a host star) in our galaxy alone. According to the Drake equation, the chances of intelligent life with advanced technological capabilities having existed or existing in the universe are dependent on various factors, including the lifespan of such civilisations. They may have existed in the past but not now (Woodruff Sullivan, University of Washington).

The fact is, we don't really know and can only work on the laws of probability. Sullivan concludes, "It is astonishingly likely that we are not the only time and place that an advance civilization has evolved." Without wishing to throw too many numbers at my readers, it is obvious that by these calculations, there should be life on at least one other planet in our galaxy alone, to say nothing of the rest of the universe, observable or otherwise. However, until now, no evidence of intelligent life beyond our planet has been detected.

As a young boy, I remember looking into the dark night sky from a Boys' Brigade campsite on the Isle of Wight, when a senior officer asked me this question: "Can you possibly imagine that there is not life somewhere out there?" Because of the sheer size of the observable universe alone and the numerical chance of intelligent life existing beyond the earth (in one or more of an estimated 100 to 200 billion galaxies), I was moved to think that that was most probably the case. Why should I have thought otherwise? At that early stage of my life, I was not as familiar with the numbers as I am now and, anyway, did not wish to disagree with a much-respected officer! He happened to be the President of our East Surrey Battalion.

Is there anyone there?

According to the laws of probability, we would expect there to be intelligent life in other regions of the universe. Recent images from both the Hubble and James Webb telescopes confirm that there are planets orbiting stars in our own galaxy within the so-called *Goldilocks Zone*, the habitable region around a star offering the right temperature for life to exist. This does not mean that other necessary requirements, such as carbon, water, and a breathable atmosphere, are present on those planets. But if there is life elsewhere in the universe, our current knowledge is that such life is of a rudimentary nature, and certainly not in the form of intelligent life or sophisticated aliens, as depicted in science fiction books and films.

The 1960s TV series, Star Trek, introduced to a human audience, members of alien races, including the likes of half human, half Vulcan, Mr Spock, and Data, an android possessed of artificial intelligence but of human appearance. These were interstellar technologically advanced species from the galaxy of which our sun is a part. Within the relative nearness of our own solar system, we know that some of the vital elements for the existence of life, past or present, do or did exist. However, in terms of interstellar space even with our latest technology, we have no evidence of the existence of advanced civilisations, similar or otherwise, to the fictional characters portrayed in Star Trek and encountered by the intrepid crew of the Starship Enterprise.

The same could be said for the 1970s franchise, Star Wars, an intergalactic portrayal of the universe, even more adventurous than its predecessor. I think the general opinion among astronomers and cosmologists is that our chances of contacting, let alone meeting, life forms comparable to Homo sapiens is extremely remote. As we cannot definitively rule out this possibility, only put forward degrees of probability, we must leave this door open, for the present, at least. It is of interest, nonetheless, to observe that our human imagination invariably leads us to invent alien forms different from ourselves, and it is perhaps of concern that artificial intelligence is now being developed in scientific laboratories and applied in various practical ways. It appears that if we cannot find alien life forms beyond our planet, at least we can create them right here on Earth! Human imagination knows no bounds and will keep pushing the frontiers of what is deemed possible towards new horizons, incorporating new inventiveness. As in the past, many as the positives may be, our ingenuity could well come back to bite us.

With the passing of the decades since that night staring into the starry sky, to my way of thinking now, the possibility of other intelligent life forms existing somewhere in the remoteness of the universe raises more questions than it answers. This seems to be true, at least from a theological perspective. Here are some of those questions:

Does God interest himself in these if they do exist?
Do they have the same need of redemption as we do?
If so, what would be God's way of dealing with this?
And what would the role of Jesus be in their redemption?
Is the salvation plan the same for other intelligent life?
How many times would Jesus need to be crucified or such like?
Was his *once and for all* sacrifice sufficient for those in need of salvation in other parts of the universe?
Or are we more privileged than we first thought?
Is ours the only planet in the universe where there is life, as we know it?
Is God's love and provision directed towards us alone?

The real Wow factor

Our own individual existence in the world is, itself, a miracle, so great are the odds against it, in what is a very random process of natural selection. Even so, it is not meaningless. Every human being, though sharing many characteristics with other human beings, is quite unique. Having written this, I came across some thoughts expressed by Joseph Ratzinger in his book, Jesus of Nazareth, in which he maintains that we are all different and the product of God's volition (see p.138). So, the seemingly random process why which we are selected at our conception may not be so random at all. We are all *chosen* by God.

But could planet Earth be as unique and *chosen* as we are? I think that may be true, although, until now, the uniqueness of Earth has not been proved. As conclusive proof is not found upon the lack of evidence, we cannot now venture any further towards a definitive answer to the question, Are we alone? What is more, we may never have the answer to this tantalising question. But I could be right and, who knows, one day you may be able to say that you have read a book by someone who said that all along, that we humans are unique throughout the realms of time and space, and that the earth is unique in its ability to birth and sustain intelligent life. At worst, I could be wrong, in which case you will kindly remain silent about this!

But, to proceed, as I write, it has been reported across the planet by international news agencies that other new worlds have been discovered orbiting a distant star in our galaxy. This has been described as the *perfect solar system* owing to the incredibly synchronised orbits of the six member planets, which are also similar in size relative to each other. This newly discovered planetary system is 100 light years from earth, and it will be a decade before we know if there are life forms on any of these planets. However, this is considered by scientists to be most unlikely as none are, temperature-wise, the right distance from their host star. They would all be far too hot to support life, as we know it.

This generated a deep sense of disappointment on my part so, despite the questions I raised earlier, I would prefer to maintain an open mind on these important matters, as in others, also. To put the final nail into the coffin of this interplanetary speculation, these newly discovered celestial bodies are gas planets and, therefore, do not have a solid surface.

To complicate matters even more, if there were intelligent life on one of these planets, it would not be possible for us to communicate across such huge distances. And depending on their technology, they might not be able to distinguish our radio signals from the noise of cosmic microwave background radiation, the afterglow following the birth of the universe.

Despite these negative findings, the existence of extra-terrestrial life, even intelligent life, is given credence by some eminent scientists, including the late Professor Stephen Hawking. According to the different views of our scientists, the possible disposition of these alien forms towards humans, ranges from benevolence to hostility. It may be to our relief or disappointment to learn that there are no signs of *little green Martians* on our neighbouring planet. And, further, all the remaining planets in our solar system have been officially ruled out as harbouring intelligent life.

As we know already, the closest star to our sun, Proxima Centauri, is 4.24 light years away, about 25 trillion miles (25,000.000.000.000 miles). The next star after ours appears even further away when its distance from Earth is seen in numbers! According to the website earthsky.org, it is home to at least two planets. Despite knowing of their existence, it would be difficult within the limitations of our present space technology to ascertain whether there is life on these or other more distant planets. Radio telescopes have yet to pick up a signal emanating from a life source in any other part of the far reaches of the universe. Moreover, no other intelligent life-form has yet been able to contact us.

Of course, we cannot rule out the possibility of extraterrestrial life, however remote that possibility might be, for lack of evidence alone. But I think the most probable scenario is that, to all intents and purposes, we are alone in the universe. At least, I would hardly argue for the existence of alien forms of intelligent life as depicted in works of science fiction.

The foregoing has been included here, to acknowledge the different views and expectations of alien life either in our own galaxy or beyond. It serves neither to prove nor disprove the existence of extraterrestrial intelligent life. But it serves as a context for my own thinking about these things.

Another relevant context is theological. If God made humans, each one unique, in his own image, and if there is only one God and creator of the universe, is it conceivable that he would also create little green men of semi-grotesque appearance with their brains on the outside of their skulls and levels of intelligence comparable or superior to our own? The longer it takes our astronomers and their radio telescopes to find intelligent life on other planets, the more likely, I feel our uniqueness will have to be assumed.

Having said that, the thought that we may be alone, makes our existence on planet Earth even more staggering than the idea that intelligent life may exist or might have existed on another planet. This may also prompt the big *Why* question. Why are we here? The answer to that can only ultimately be found in the context of God's existence and his purposes for us, and the planet we call home.

Shortly before he died, Stephen Hawking, speaking on the National Geographic Star Talk programme, said that the universe was not something formed from nothing. He also spoke of the horizontal dimension of time, past and present, and the vertical dimension before the big bang when time, as we know it, did not exist. This would seem to suggest two possibilities: firstly, that before the universe came into existence, matter of some kind already existed, and therefore we have the reality of prior existence. Secondly, in relation to the vertical dimension, the concept, not of time but eternity, before time existed. Professor Hawking, if not in so many words, appears to accept the realities of prior existence and eternity. This would sit comfortably with the account of how everything began as recorded in the first chapter of Genesis. Having made his statement about existence before the universe, Hawking then realised that he had opened the door to the possibility of a divine creator and immediately went in search of another theory to show that the universe had no beginning and could be explained without the need for a Creator; thereby attempting to close the door to that possibility.

Writing a summary of Hawking's book, A Brief History of Time, Elizabeth Whitworth comments, as follows: "Hawking felt that further theoretical development was needed to scientifically (that is, without invoking a divine creator who could arbitrarily fine-tune the universe for the benefit of humankind) explain how the universe came to be the way it is." (Shortform Books).

It is understandable that as a prominent scientist, Professor Hawking was anxious for science to provide the answer to this huge question, and for this we can be grateful. To complement this, it is also noteworthy that our attempts to dispense with God, for whatever reason, emanate from the first garden and lie at the heart of original sin (see Joseph Ratzinger, Jesus of Nazareth, pp.138-39). It should not surprise us, then, that this tendency is prevalent today, particularly in the affluent Western Europe, where many seem to have outgrown their need or love of God.

We have seen already that lack of evidence is not a proof per se. The same can be said of God. Though there is evidence both from the natural world and from the personal experience of individuals and communities this is not always accepted, on the basis that it is unverifiable, according to the scientific approach.

Good bedfellows

Although there is evidence for the existence of God, both from the natural world and the personal experience of individuals and communities, this cannot be demonstrated scientifically. But for verifiability to be achieved a step of faith is required by both the scientific and religious communities.

You will now be familiar with the stance of this book, that science and theology are not necessarily incompatible, only if one wishes to think them so. As it so happens, I do not believe them to be incompatible at all. Nevertheless, it is fascinating to watch the scientific community, as it strives for an answer to what is still an imponderable question. How did the universe begin? The Big Bang is the best theory to date, though new theories are beginning to challenge this, such as the concept of an infinitely expanding and contracting universe.

But how far has the Big Bang theory taken us on our journey of discovery? A good distance I would say, in the region of 14.5 billion years into the past. This theory answers the question back to that point in time, the beginning of time. But before that? To this question, we still do not have an answer that measures up to standard procedures of observation, testing and verification. We are all required to take a step into the unknown which, by definition, is a step of faith. As theories can only be proven through observation and testing, the answer to this fundamental question will remain as elusive as ever. For the time being, the jury is out.

Another question still to be answered is whether there is life resembling human life elsewhere in the universe? Our astronomers have not yet been able to give us an answer to that question as hard as they search for one. There is also nothing in the Bible to suggest that God may have other projects elsewhere in the universe. There is much said in the Bible about the heavens above and around us and how they declare the glory of God, but no indication that there are alien creatures or species, or even those like us, on other planets orbiting distant stars. By distant I mean distances that we are unlikely ever to traverse.

To make matters worse, scientists believe that the universe is expanding at an increasing rate, due to the presence and influence of mysterious dark matter (see Robert S. White, <u>Science and Christianity</u>, pp.138-39). The result is that many celestial objects that we cannot already see will fall beyond the observable horizon, forever. In this scenario, it will never be possible to observe the entire universe, let alone travel across it.

Putting all of this into a *local* perspective, for humans to travel to the nearest star to our sun would take a staggering 81.000 years, even with our most advanced technological capabilities, to date. Although stars within individual galaxies are not actually moving away in relation to each other, to cover such a distance in a single lifetime would clearly be impossible. The implications of this stark reality are now becoming increasingly apparent. Given that intelligent life, comparable to Homo sapiens, could exist out there, it is unlikely we will ever know. And it is even less likely we will ever meet our celestial neighbours across distances which are measured in light years, because there are simply too many noughts to comprehend.

But never say *No*. This may come as a disappointment to many but, as I have already argued, it serves to accentuate the extraordinariness and wonder of our own planet, of our own existence and the huge privilege that is ours of being here on this unique celestial sphere. As always, great privilege brings great responsibility and especially in the way we relate to the natural world, and to our fellow human beings.

This brings us to the important question of personal and corporate accountability, as stewards of this unique finite place in the universe. A world in which, from a scientific point of view, we happen to find ourselves, or from the vantage point of faith, where we have been placed by God.

What can we do?

By all accounts, there is considerable scope for the investment of time and resources in the way we manage the affairs of the planet. Inequality, injustice, and the uneven distribution of wealth are all conditions and situations within the province and control of the stewards of Earth's resources. It is incumbent on us, also, to conserve and replenish those very resources on which we all depend for our own futures and those of our children and our children's children, throughout successive future generations.

Carl Sagan, the American scientist with close involvement in the Voyager I and 2 missions, provides us with a rude awakening regarding our present situation and, also, a timely reminder of the cosmic context in which we all find ourselves today:

"Our planet is a lonely speck in the great enveloping cosmic dark. In our obscurity, in all this vastness, there is no hint that help will come from elsewhere to save us from ourselves. The Earth is the only world known so far to harbour life" (Pale Blue Dot quotes from Goodreads).

As I have said in another of my books, Encounters with God in Brazil, it is not so important what we do in this world or achieve for ourselves, but what we leave behind and pass onto others that really matters. It is the difference we make to their lives and the future of their respective communities that is our truly authentic contribution to the world and to the kingdom of God on Earth. We can all make a positive difference where there is the will to do so, and if we can agree to work together to achieve the goals that belong to our common interests. By being the expression of the inbreaking of God's kingdom, by being in tune with God's will and doing God's will, we shall hasten the return of Jesus and the inauguration of the new Earth for which this earth is waiting. This means, among other things, looking to the immediate and longer-term needs of others, being kinder to one another, caring for the resources God has provided for us and with which he has so graciously blessed us, and as part and parcel of these attitudes and activities, proclaiming the Good News of the gospel *from Jerusalem to the end of the earth* (Acts 1:8).

The key words in Scripture regarding the Parousia seem to me to be those spoken by Jesus, himself, as recorded in the Gospel of Mark: "And the gospel must first be preached to all the nations" (13:10).

The obvious way to advance the cause of the gospel is to live it out day by day. Effective witness to the life, death, and resurrection of Jesus must be seen to be believed. St. Francis of Assisi has stated plainly what is required and where that begins:

"Lord, make me an instrument of your peace: where there is hatred, *let me sow* love; where there is injury, pardon; where there is doubt, faith; where there is despair, hope; where there is darkness, light; where there is sadness, joy" (my italics).

This kind of altruism though epitomised in the life and work of St. Francis did not actually originate with him, but is found as long ago as two millennia, in the Old Testament prophets Amos, Hosea, and

Micah. Through these ancient seers God spoke to the divided kingdom of Israel, north as well as south. On behalf of these, Micah speaks both succinctly and eloquently:

> He has shown you, O man, what is good; and what does the Lord require of you. But to do justly, to love mercy, and to walk humbly with your God (6:8).

This, I believe, is the essence of all true religion and something clearly enshrined in, and central to, the life and teaching of Jesus:

> Love the Lord your God with all your heart, with all your soul, and with all your mind; and your neighbour as yourself (Matthew 22:37-40).

A personal relationship with Jesus, as it so happens, is also a personal relationship with God, the creator of heaven and earth. Our relationship with Jesus allows us to see the indelible stamp of the Creator imprinted upon his work in creation:

> The heavens declare the glory of God; and the firmament shows his handiwork. Day unto day utters speech, and night unto night reveals knowledge. There is no speech nor language where their voice is not heard (Psalm 19:1-3).

If we allow his works to speak to us, they will also reveal him to us. Because of our relationship with God through Jesus, we will see as we gaze into the night sky not only the stars and planets in their glorious array but, more than this, the One who made these far distant celestial objects and assembled them for his delight. It is not until then that we are able to express true wonder and awe.

God's piece de resistance, his masterpiece, however, is the creation of man and woman. If we place our human uniqueness alongside a growing awareness of the uniqueness of the earth, we achieve the perfect partnership that brings joy and satisfaction to God's heart. The setting of man and woman in a garden (a paradisal garden that provided abundantly for all their needs) is where we began this book. But it ends with God's vision of a new Earth and a glorious city coming out of heaven.

This new Earth will be his dwelling place, his new creation, restored and redeemed, in the same way that we ourselves are redeemed. It is at the cross that we discover and experience our true need, and in the city of God that we can be our true selves among the people of God. Because in both these sacred places, we find ourselves in the loving presence of the One who is the Author of life in all its forms and, also, life eternal.

For further personal reflection or group discussion:

What do you feel are the chances of finding extra-terrestrial life?

What do you think might be God's plan for intelligent life elsewhere in the universe?

If Earth is unique and if there is no other life supporting planet in the universe, how does that make you feel about yourself and the rest of the planet?

How do you think science and Christian belief can work together toward a better understanding of the universe?

What should be our personal priorities as inhabitants of planet Earth?

CHAPTER SEVEN
CAN I BELIEVE?

Refreshing and new ways of thinking and reasoning are seldom hit upon randomly or in isolation. Quite often, it would seem, different thinkers are simultaneously pondering the same subject from the same or different perspective, but none to their knowledge are directly influenced by the others. However, there is probably a common link to these thought-patterns as they develop. So what have we discovered on this journey together? In writing these pages, I have been surprised to see that I am in excellent company when it comes to where I now find myself. This may well be explained from a passage of the New Testament which reads as follows:

> We also have the prophetic word made more sure, which you do well to heed as to a light that shines in a dark place, until the day dawns and the morning star rises in your hearts; knowing this first, that no prophecy of Scripture is of any private interpretation, for prophecy never came by the will of man, but holy men of God spoke as they were moved by the Holy Spirit (2 Peter 1:19-21).

God, through his Spirit, implants in our hearts and minds his own thoughts, so that we may share these with one another. Paul said: "For I received from the Lord that which I also delivered to you" (1 Corinthians 11:23).

Many scholars understand that Paul received this directive by revelation from God, which also corresponds closely to what he had declared previously:

But I make known to you, brethren, that the gospel which was preached by me is not according to man. For I neither received it from man, nor was I taught it, but it came through the revelation of Jesus Christ (Galatians 1:11-12).

It should be remembered that Paul's letters to the Galatian and Corinthian churches were written before the gospel accounts of the life and ministry of Jesus. Therefore, some important theology (more precisely Christology) appeared in written form before the related historical accounts or background.

The earliest creeds were also written before the Gospels, which is significant, as I will explain in a moment. The authorship of the earliest gospel document is not known but deals with the sayings of Jesus rather than the historical context in which these sayings were spoken. Two of the Gospel writers turned to this anonymous document, known as, *Q* (literally, *Source*), for much of their own content. We can conclude, therefore, that the words of Jesus were remembered and recorded before a description of their historical setting was written down. The teaching of Jesus would have largely been preserved in its earliest form by way of an oral tradition, based on the recollections of those who were present at the time and had witnessed the occasions of his teaching first-hand, or who had heard on the *grapevine* as the stories concerning Jesus and what he taught were passed down. There is no reason that I can see, to suggest that the stories are not based on reliable witness testimony.

Papias of Hierapolis (c. 60-c. 130 AD), has it that Mark wrote down the recollections of Peter of whom, it is believed, he was a disciple, and Luke (by his own testimony) researched diligently into these things when preparing his version of events (Luke 1:1-4). Both Matthew and Luke make considerable use of material from Mark, the earliest written Gospel, and John, even if we make the concession that he did not actually write the Fourth Gospel, himself, was still alive until the end of the first century, when it was written. The personal references in John's Gospel to the *other disciple* (20:8) and, also, the *disciple Jesus loved* (13:23) are clear indications that he wrote the Gospel or collaborated in its writing, or was known to the writer.

Jesus of history

The historical-critical method of interpreting the Bible has given rise in more recent times to the so-called quest for the historical Jesus, a movement which posed doubts as to the historical reliability of the Gospel accounts of the life and ministry of Jesus. This movement, however, did not go so far as to question the existence of Jesus. His crucifixion is, in fact, recorded in extra-biblical literature of the late 1st and early 2nd centuries namely, The Antiquities of the Jews by Josephus, and Annals, a record kept by the Roman senator and historian, Tacitus. The problem has been whether we can genuinely know the real Jesus of Nazareth, as a historical figure, within the social and cultural setting of first-century Palestine.

This has subsequently led to an emphasis on the Christ of faith and a relevant contemporary experience of Christ as our risen and exalted Lord. This alternative approach to knowing Jesus and relating to him is also based on affirmations regarding the person and continuing work of Jesus, as they are set out in the Pauline epistles and elsewhere in the New Testament.

And it is perfectly right, of course, that we should be encouraged in this way. Indeed, this is how we are supposed to relate to Jesus today, through the activity of the Holy Spirit in our lives. This is how Jesus said it would be: "And I will pray the Father, and he will give you another Helper, that he may abide with you forever" (John 14:16).

Nevertheless, I would again defend the reliability of much of the historical setting and context for the life and ministry of Jesus, on the basis that Mark, the earliest Gospel, was written a relatively short period of 35-40 years after the crucifixion and resurrection, when many of the first-hand witnesses were still alive. Most notably, Peter was alive until 64 AD, and John right up to the end of the first century. Also, James, the brother of Jesus, lived until the 60s AD.

Joseph Ratzinger is right in pointing out that these pillars of the church would have vouched for the authenticity of the traditions of the Gospel circulating at that time (Jesus of Nazareth, p.297). These, of all people, would have had no interest or reason that we can imagine, for allowing layers of errant tradition to obscure the objective facts of the gospel, as they personally recalled them. John and Peter, of course, were not only of the Twelve, they were also of the three in whom Jesus most confided the mystery of his person.

I can see no other reason why they would have laid down their lives for a cause unless it had impacted them in ways as nothing else ever had. We know that James, the brother of Jesus, was not a believer until after the event of the resurrection. Paul informs us that Jesus appeared to James, which is highly relevant, insofar as James became the leader of the Jerusalem church. These are facts that fit together into a coherent whole and make sense as we look at them together and not in isolation. As it so happened, with the rise of state instigated persecution aimed directly at the followers of Jesus, especially their leaders, it would have been natural and logical that the Gospel was committed to writing for it to survive in the long-term and, in the providence of God, for generations to come.

It is also important to understand that at that time in Palestine rabbinical teaching was traditionally transmitted orally and committed to memory by their students and hearers. Jesus, himself, taught this way, and his frequent use of parables would have facilitated greatly the ability of the people to retain and recall the words he had spoken. Because of this, the minds of the people would have been trained to memorise to good effect not only the teaching of Jesus, but also the stories they had heard about Jesus from others. These same stories were then written down for the purpose of preserving the narrative concerning the historical person of Jesus, as he was known to the Galilean fishermen, whom he called to follow him.

In his quest to discover the historical figure of Jesus, Joseph Ratzinger reminds us how Jesus sought communion with the Father after a busy day preaching and healing. Also significantly before choosing his disciples. Such moments as these are windows into the personal life of Jesus, divest of the subsequent layers of tradition which some scholars feel have obscured our view of who he really was and what he was really like.

The parables offer another window on the world of that time. These give us a close-up of Jesus and the world in which he lived and taught. However, there are various factors to be considered when using the parables as windows on their life setting, including their use and adaptation by the primitive church, as explained by J. Jeremias in his <u>The Parables of Jesus</u>. Even in their original context, the meaning of these *stories from life* was not immediately understood, not even by those closest to Jesus. Nevertheless, the sayings of Jesus are to take priority over the secondary importance of their historical setting.

The fact that the written Gospels came later would indicate that, to begin with, priority was given to the immediate practical and spiritual needs of the primitive church, rather than to dwell on the historical setting within which Jesus lived in Palestine. The letters to the churches which we can attribute to Paul were written before even the earliest of the four gospels. The gospel stories, as we know them today, came into circulation as the written versions of them appeared. To reach a conclusion as to how much these stories can be relied on for an authentic picture of Jesus of Nazareth, we should bear in mind the later post-resurrection tradition of the church and its relation to the written Gospels.

As significant first-hand witnesses were still alive and able to corroborate the stories told in the written gospels, there seems to be no reason for seriously doubting their authenticity. To my mind there is even less reason to assume that our only knowledge of Jesus is that derived from later reflection on the part of the church, which was superimposed on the Gospel narrative. Allowing for further theological development regarding the person of Jesus and the nature of his relationship to God the Father should not cause us to be forgetful of the earlier traditions passed on by word of mouth, in connection with the teaching and miracles of Jesus, his death and resurrection. Such matters were amply discussed at church councils in Nicaea in 325 AD and Chalcedon in 451 AD.

I would mention here that the Fourth Gospel is different from the Synoptic Gospels in its focus and presentation, tending to dwell on the significance of the person of Jesus rather than the historical ordering of the day-to-day events themselves. I would not wish to infer that this Gospel is in any way ahistorical - not at all. There are numerous times, in fact, when the circumstances and historical context of John's account bear the marks of a first-hand witness. For example, at the wedding in Cana, an event to which all the disciples were invited (2:1-12) and the miraculous catch of fish, where John is clearly mentioned among those of the disciples who were present on this occasion (21:1-14). To these we could add the *checking-out* visit to the empty tomb on Easter Sunday, by Peter and *the other disciple*, which is widely understood to be a reference to John himself.

In each of these stories, it is quite clear that John is giving his own personal commentary from the point of view of one who was present at the time (20:1-10). Furthermore, the Apostle John is categorical that he was a witness to the crucifixion, that he has told the truth as to exactly what took place that day, and that by the loss of water and blood from Jesus' side, he had died on the cross that afternoon (John 19:35). Altogether, there is firm ground for accepting the historical reliability of John's Gospel, as well as those of the synoptic writers, the reasons for which we have given above.

This brief backcloth to the traditions also provides the ground for believing in the future Jesus has promised to all those who follow him. Notwithstanding the importance of the historical rootedness of the gospels for knowing Jesus as he was known to the first disciples, I would reiterate that it is right and proper for us to focus on Jesus as he is now and how he relates to us today. It is important that we move forward in our relationship with the risen, exalted Christ, without turning away from the historical person of Jesus who will always be fundamental for our core belief that God is *with us*.

What we know now

What, then, has God revealed to us on our journey through this book? Traditional views of heaven are deeply embedded in our human psyche. The idea that heaven is above and a long way above, at the end of a final, long journey of the soul, is common to many religions.

This idea is derived from our use of language rather than biblical and theological considerations. The advances in the exploration of space, its vastness and emptiness, have not diminished our belief in heaven as our ultimate destination. Yuri Gagarin, the Russian cosmonaut and first man to orbit the earth, is given to have said, after he returned from space in 1961, that he did not see God while high above in orbit round the earth. It now appears that these words were attributed to the cosmonaut by Nikita Khrushchev, in a derisive comment to discredit Christian belief in a personal God. Apparently, Gagarin was a man of faith throughout his life. In my book, Jesus: Dead or Alive? The evidence, I responded to his supposed declaration about not finding God in space by saying that he was possibly looking in the wrong place.

In this present book, I have sought to identify where heaven is and how it will play out. Another answer to Yuri Gagarin, or whoever spoke those famous words on his behalf, is that God is spirit and, therefore, invisible to human eyes or photographic lenses, including those of the highest definition. My aim here has been to listen to what the Bible is saying to us, as we bear in mind that the language of the Bible comes from a time when words were used differently to describe our understanding of the world and the cosmos in general.

Even our own use of language today, when talking about these matters, may also be outdated. For example, when we speak of heaven being somewhere *up in the sky* or of Jesus being 'taken up' into heaven, when it is inaccurate to refer to the cosmos in this way. This does not mean that we are denying the existence of heaven or the reality of the Ascension, for that matter. Far from it! God's all-pervading presence is everywhere around us; and heaven is where God is.

The other reason for believing that heaven is not in some non-material realm is that when Jesus rose from the dead, he was still clothed in a physical body, albeit of a strikingly different nature to that before his resurrection.

Ruth Valerio, in Say Yes to Life, has rightly drawn attention to the idea that our spiritual body is still a body, as does Tom Wright who says, in a similar vein, that "the new world will be more real, more physically solid, than the present one" (New Heavens, New Earth, p.14). This may not quite tally with traditional views of heaven, but when we look at Scripture more closely, a new reality comes into focus.

The Apostle Paul draws important parallels between Jesus' resurrection body and our own future glorified bodies:

> There is one glory of the sun, another glory of the moon, and another glory of the stars, for one star differs from another star in glory. So, also, is the resurrection of the dead. The body is sown in corruption; it is raised in *incorruption*. It is sown in dishonour; it is raised in glory. It is sown in weakness; it is raised in power. It is sown a natural body; it is raised a spiritual body. There is a natural body, and there is a spiritual body (1 Corinthians 15:41-44).

There is also a close connection between our glorified bodies and the transformed heaven and earth. The two go together. Our new bodies will be perfectly suited to our new environment. This is carried forward into our connectedness and affinity with the risen Lord: "As we have borne the image of the man of dust, we shall also bear the image of the heavenly man" (1 Corinthians 15:49).

We will not only be in the presence of the Lord we will also be acutely aware of his presence with us and of ourselves in his presence, in ways not possible in our present earthly state.

It is by looking at all the relevant texts that we come to our considered conclusions. We have intentionally refrained from fanciful thoughts, so as not to be led up the wrong paths when it comes to how and where God's heavenly rule will be enacted.

The planet today and tomorrow

The impressive, unequalled spectacle of Earth's blue orb, suspended in the blackness of infinite space, inevitably draws our attention like nothing seen from the planet's surface. Those who have been privileged to set foot on our only natural satellite, the Moon, say that this is the most strikingly memorable vista that ever their eyes have set upon. Out on its own, a candidate in pole position, for God's choice for his heaven.

I have stood many times on Corcovado Mountain, high above the Brazilian city of Rio de Janeiro. From this vantage point, the city below is constantly under the gaze of Christ the Redeemer, whose statue is now one of the seven wonders of the modern world. As I stood there, I marvelled at the panorama stretched out before me; of distant shorelines and tiny boats moored in the shelter of Sugar Loaf Mountain. The sight draws and inspires the human spirit from deep within. This is surely a leading contender for one of the world's most beautiful and imposing views, one which epitomises our amazing blue planet. That is, until one descends to the sleazy nondescript backstreets of the city below, where crime and danger lurk. Not everywhere, of course, but enough to stand in stark contrast to the allure of the vista as seen from the mountaintop.

This, I would dare to suggest, is a microcosm of planet Earth. God's doing and Man's undoing. To put it another way, we can imagine Eden but only from afar, as a distant reality. What is much nearer now is a world awaiting the closing act of God's redemptive drama, the coming of the Son of Man on the clouds of heaven.

And we are given a glimpse of what this will mean for us, as seen by the disciple who leaned on Jesus' breast:

> Behold, the tabernacle of God is with men, and he will dwell with them, and they shall be his people, and God himself will be with them and be their God (Revelation 21:3).

George Eldon Ladd is most helpful in explaining to us the significance of this brief glimpse through the curtain of heaven, which I shall resume as follows. It was, he says, in previous times, the element of continuity with God's covenant promise to Abraham, Moses, and David, but now, because of the New Covenant, ratified in the blood of the Lamb, the redeemed will see God's face (Revelation 22:4). This is the joy and glory of the New Earth, the centre of which is the New Jerusalem. This is the long-term objective of God's redemptive purposes in human history; that God should dwell among his people and that they should see his face. This is, second to none, the greatest blessing of all (Teologia do Novo Testamento, pp.838-39).

The prophet Isaiah foresaw this amazing new reality from far back in Old Testament days:

> For behold, I create new heavens and a new earth; and the former shall not be remembered or come to mind. But be glad and rejoice forever in what I create. For

> behold, I create Jerusalem as a rejoicing, and her people a joy. I will rejoice in Jerusalem, and joy in my people; the voice of weeping shall no longer be heard in her, nor the voice of crying (Isaiah 65:17-19).

The words of the prophet bear a striking resemblance to those of the Apostle John in his apocalyptic vision of a future without tears, pain, sorrow, and death. Heaven and earth will be so transformed and infinitely better than the former, that the old will no longer be missed or even remembered.

There is also a welcome state of permanency about the new heaven and earth:

> For as the new heavens and the new earth which I shall make shall remain before me, says the Lord, so shall your descendants and your name remain (Isaiah 66:22).

The theme of a new heaven and a new earth pervades the whole of Scripture, as does the deep-rooted message of assurance and of hope in a future of blessing where God receives the grateful service and ceaseless worship of his people. To use an analogy from Jesus' own lips, the tares will be separated from the wheat, and pain and sorrow will no longer exist, because the cause of these will have been banished from sight for ever (Matthew 13:36-43).

There are those who have mocked the idea that Jesus will return at all. There is also a sincerely held view that Jesus was mistaken when he indicated to his disciples that the Parousia would happen within their lifetime:

Immediately after the tribulation of those days the sun will be darkened, and the moon will not give its light; the stars will fall from heaven, and the powers of the heavens will be shaken... and they will see the Son of Man coming on the clouds of heaven with power and great glory. Assuredly, I say to you, this generation will by no means pass away till all these things are fulfilled (Matthew 24:29, 30b, 34).

The Apostle Peter addresses this apparent non-event in his second letter (3.1-13) and asserts that the supposed delay is due to God's patience, so that none should perish but that all should come to repentance. This depicts an overwhelmingly just and merciful God for whom there is no pleasure in the consequences of sin. Paul reiterates this same view when writing to the church in Thessalonica: "For God did not appoint us to wrath, but to obtain salvation through our Lord Jesus Christ" (1 Thessalonians 5:9).

George Beasley-Murray, a deeply committed evangelical scholar, with a powerful intellect and a heart to win others for Christ, in a lecture to his students, raised the possibility that Jesus may have been mistaken regarding the timing of his return. This does not give up on the idea of the Parousia but rather affirms that it is yet to happen. Jesus may, in fact, have been pointing to another cataclysmic event, namely the destruction of Jerusalem, together with all its state and religious institutions, at the hands of the Romans in AD 70. Indeed, did he not foresee this and speak about this with great sorrow on his entry into Jerusalem on Palm Sunday?

In the Gospel of Matthew, the words of Jesus concerning the timing of his return to earth, form part of the parable of the fig tree, which is to be found among several other predictions in the same chapter, including the dramatic scenes surrounding the destruction of the temple (Matthew 24:1-2). Matthew also tends to present his material in an organised and didactical fashion, and it could be that it is his arrangement of the sayings of Jesus rather than the words themselves that present us with the difficulties we encounter here.

Whatever conclusions we may come to regarding the *Parousia*, the consensus would perhaps be around the position taken by Peter whom Jesus set apart as pastor of the flock. He had witnessed, as part of the inner circle of disciples, such watershed moments as the Transfiguration of Jesus and many others. Peter had matured a great deal by the time he wrote his second general letter to the churches. No longer impulsive, it would seem, but now in a position to give a considered response to those who had doubts about the timing of this critical event in human history. Could this assurance have been given by one with a more intimate knowledge of Jesus and his patient forbearing with those who fall short, than the Apostle Peter?

Though the actual order of events associated with the end times may not be fully understood, we have identified the events themselves, which are the Parousia, the resurrection of the saints, the Millennium, the new heaven and earth and, finally, the New Jerusalem coming down out of heaven from God. None of this runs contrary to the prospect of God's heavenly rule being established on Earth, or even the ultimate destruction of earth, as it is engulfed by our dying sun:

> And there shall be no night there: They need no lamp nor light of the sun, for the Lord God gives them light. And they shall reign forever and ever (Revelation 22:5).

This biblical affirmation is perfectly echoed in the words of a popular hymn, written on 6 January 1859, to celebrate Epiphany:

In the heavenly country bright,
need they no created light.
Thou its light, its joy, its crown,
thou its sun, which goes not down.
There forever may we sing,
Hallelujahs to our King.

'As with gladness men of old'
W. C. Dix

The words of this hymn do not part company with either the Bible or with science. In fact, they agree with science and, at the same time, take us beyond science. These words and the Bible passage on which they are based do something which science cannot do and does not pretend to do. They offer the hope and assurance that the divine image in us, and the hopeful awareness that springs from it, will not be frustrated or disappointed, even when our local star has set below the horizon for the last time.

Against a constant daily backcloth of bad news besetting us from all sides, and the continual barrage of the voices of the prophets of doom, this is good news!

There are clear prophetic voices speaking to us from the Bible, to which we might and should give heed. Many of these prophecies have already come to pass, but there are others that are waiting their turn, even as we speak. Some of these happenings we may have witnessed in our lifetime, and we might have wondered if they were the fulfilment of the ancient prophecies. One thing is certain, when the Lord does come, he will do so at a time we least expect.

As I draw my thoughts to a close, may I remind you of these words of Jesus. They were recorded by John Mark, whose family most likely owned the house of the Upper Room, which became a regular meeting-place for the apostles:

> But of that day and hour no one knows, neither the angels in heaven, nor the Son, but only the Father. Take heed, watch, and pray. For you do not know when the time is. It is like a man going to a far country, who left his house and gave authority to his servants, and to each his work, and commanded the doorkeeper to watch. Watch therefore, for you do not know when the master of the house is coming – in the evening, at midnight, at the crowing of the cock, or in the morning – lest, coming suddenly, he finds you sleeping. And what I say to you, I say to all - Watch! (Mark 13:32-37).

For that generation, as for every generation, it is our God-given task to be vigilant and watchful, observant of the signs that are constantly around us in one form or another. In our own generation, as the present stewards of this celestial sphere, we are called to walk in step with God's vision for its future. We are here to make a difference to the world to make it a better place for all its inhabitants. Because God undoubtedly has a heart for this planet, we should take special care of it now.

And as we assume and carry forward the privilege of this sacred task, so the day of his return draws inexorably nearer, when heaven and earth will again become one. As in the first garden.

Amen.

Even so, come, Lord Jesus!

For further personal reflection or group discussion:

How does God speak to us today? Do you hear him speaking to you?

Can we know Jesus as his first disciples knew him? Is this important for our faith in him today?

What does Paul have to say about our spiritual bodies? How different will these be from our earthly body?

How does the Apostle Peter explain the apparent delay in Jesus' return to earth?

If no one except the Father knows the hour of Jesus' return, how can we prepare for this cosmic event?

POSTSCRIPT

The experience of writing this account of the end times and how they will pan out was like placing a sheet of photographic paper into a developing tray. The submerged image of my disconnected and sometimes random thoughts had been impressed on light-sensitive paper from an original negative using a red safe lamp. As the developer did its work on the paper, so an image slowly appeared. This, it seems to me, serves as an appropriate analogy of what happened during the final organisation of the original material.

As I finalised the chapter titles and reduced these from an original ten to seven chapters so, miraculously, a picture emerged before my eyes, as with a photographic image as it shimmers in the developing tray.

This book began its journey with an intellectual and emotional response to a photograph, the first ever taken of the entire sphere of planet Earth. The subsequent writing process and arrangement of the material presented here has been a learning curve towards, what is for me personally, a clearer understanding of the present and future relationship of heaven and earth.

PPS.

News has just come in that an alien life form may have been trying to contact planet Earth. We do not know yet if they are aware of our location in the universe, or if they are friendly or hostile. We can only wait and see; and hope and pray that they come in peace!

BIBLIOGRAPHY

D. Alexander, Creation or Evolution: Do we have to choose? Monarch Books. Oxford. 2008

_____, Life Sciences. In: The Lion Handbook of Science and Christianity. Ed. R. J. Berry. Lion. Oxford. 2012

G.R. Beasley-Murray, The Revelation, The New Bible Commentary Revised, Eds. D. Guthrie et al. Inter-Varsity Press. London. 1970

D. J. Bosch Transforming Mission: Paradigm Shifts in Theology of Mission. Orbis Books. Maryknoll, New York. 1991

F. F. Bruce, The Epistle of Paul to the Romans, Tyndale Press. London. 1963

G. Campbell, Breaking Through and Reaching Out, Book 2, Kingdom Publishers. London. 2022

G. Campbell Morgan, Studies in the Four Gospels. Fleming H. Revell Company. Old Tappan, NJ. 1931

W. Eaton, The Theologian in Parish Life in: The Trial of Faith. Ed. Peter Eaton. Churchman Publishing. Worthing. 1988

R. Glover, The Gospel of Matthew. Zondervan. Grand Rapids, Michigan. 1956

P. Gooder, Where on Earth is Heaven? SPCK. London. 2015

H. A. Guy, The Study of the Gospels. MacMillan. New York. 1967

R. Haldane, <u>The Epistle to the Romans</u>. Banner of Truth Trust. London. 1958

N. Hillyer, <u>1 and 2 Corinthians</u>. The New Bible Commentary Revised. Eds. D. Guthrie et al. Inter-Varsity Press. London. 1970

J. Jeremias, <u>The Parables of Jesus</u>. Revised Edition. SCM. London. 1963

R. Kivitz, <u>Quebrando Paradigmas</u>. Abba Press. São Paulo. 1998

G. E. Ladd, <u>Teologia do Novo Testamento</u>. PT. Edição Revisada. Hagnos. São Paulo. 2003

L. Morris, <u>The First Epistle of Paul to the Corinthians</u>. Tyndale Press. London. 1958

------------, <u>The Revelation of St. John</u>. Tyndale Press. London. 1969

Joseph Ratzinger, <u>Jesus of Nazareth: From the Baptism in the Jordan to the Transfiguration</u>. English Translation. Bloomsbury. London. 2007

F. A. Schaeffer, <u>Escape from Reason</u>. Inter-Varsity Press. London. 1968

N. Spencer, <u>Darwin and God</u>. SPCK. 2009

R. V. G. Tasker, <u>The Gospel According to St. John</u>. Tyndale Press. London. 1960

R. Valerio, <u>Saying Yes to Life</u>. SPCK. London. 2020

A. Weiser, <u>The Psalms</u>. SCM Press. London. 1962

R. S. White, Physical and Earth Sciences. In: The Lion Handbook of Science and Christianity. Ed. R. J. Berry. Lion. Oxford. 2012

N. T. Wright, New Heavens, New Earth: The biblical picture of Christian hope. Second Edition. Grove Books. Cambridge. 2006

_____, Surprised by Hope. SPCK. London. 2007

E. J. Young, Daniel. The New Bible Commentary Revised. Eds. D. Guthrie et al. Inter-Varsity Press. London. 1970

Articles consulted:

Jamie Carter, Pale Blue Dot. www.travelandleisure.com 22 August 2019

Stuart Clark, The Voyager mission and our Pale Blue Dot: How the most famous picture in science came to be. BBC Science Focus.sciencefocus.com 14 April 2020

Calla Cofield, Stephen Hawking: Intelligent aliens could destroy humanity, but let's search anyway. Live Science. livescience.com 21 July 2015

Simon Driver, ABC Science Are there more stars in the universe than grains of sand on Earth? www.abc.net.au 19 August 2015

Erik Gregersen, How do we know how far away the stars are? Encyclopaedia Britannica (Science and Tech). www.britannica.com

Kim Matulef, If people evolved from apes, then why are there still apes? The Tech Interactive, Stanford Medicine, Department of Genetics. www.thetech.org December 1, 2005

Gil Oliveira, Earth history in your hand. Carnegie Museum of Natural History. carnegiemnh.org/earth

Emily Osterloff, How an asteroid ended the age of the dinosaurs. Natural History Museum.nhm.ac.uk

Carl Sagan, Pale Blue Dot Quotes, sourced from Goodreads. www.goodreads.com

Toby Saunders, How many galaxies are there in the universe? BBC Science Focus. sciencefocus.com 25 July 2023

Govert Schilling, Does the universe expand faster than light? BBC Sky at Night Magazine. www.skyatnightmagazine.com 26 January 2024

Leonor Sierra, Are we alone in the universe? Revisiting the Drake equation. NASA Exoplanet Exploration. exoplanets.nasa.gov 19 May 2016

Woodruff Sullivan, University of Washington. Are we alone in the universe? Revisiting the Drake equation. NASA Exoplanet Exploration. exoplanets.nasa.gov 19 May 2016

Keith Welch, Jefferson Lab Science Education. Questions and Answers. www.education.jlab.org

Elizabeth Whitworth, What is the Singularity Theory in Physics? Shortform. shortform.com 19 February 2022

www.ingramcontent.com/pod-product-compliance
Lightning Source LLC
Chambersburg PA
CBHW071125130526
44590CB00056B/2235